7

E

SECRETS *of the* PRIMAVERSE

SECRETS *of the* PRIMAVERSE

WHY GOD CANNOT EXIST AND NOTHING CAN EXIST WITHOUT HIM

JOEL H. POSNER

METAFISICA

NEW YORK, NY

Library of Congress Number: 2012935160

ISBN 978-1-936940-24-0

Jacket design by Michael diCanio

Book production by Barbara Patterson

Metafisica in association with Epigraph Books
22 East Market Street, Suite 304, Rhinebeck, New York 12527

For Mom & Dad

TABLE
of
CONTENTS

MIND THE GOD GAP
Page 2

I. REALITY
Page 10

II. GOD
Page 52

III. TRUTH
Page 88

ESSENCE VERSUS EXISTENCE REDUX
Page 118

"It is one of the worthiest inquiries to see how far our reason can go in the knowledge of God."

— IMMANUEL KANT

MIND

the

GOD GAP

A DEBATE ONCE DISCREETLY WAGED in club chairs and smoking jackets now rages on bookstore shelves and blogs, TV and talk radio, college campuses and community school boards. This is no drawing-room dialogue about the existence of God. Everyone is taking sides, and no one is taking prisoners. The new atheists are as forthright and outspoken as the new believers squaring off against them. Exchanges are heated by the absolute confidence of clashing convictions.

The most vocal representatives on both sides of the God gap have largely and tacitly agreed on rules of engagement consistent with formal, if not civil, debate. The side that delivers the most convincing arguments supported by the most compelling evidence wins. Typical affirmative arguments call up the wonders of creation as testimony to divine manufacture and maintenance. Negative rebuttals invoke the atrocities that punctuate our history and plague our world. Believers attempt to discredit scientific theories and empirical findings, or to assign spiritual significance to them. Non-believers rush to the defense of science and denounce speculation of an unscientific nature. On and on it goes.

What perpetuates this exchange is the assumption on either side that ultimately a preponderance of evidence will effectively prove or disprove the resolution that God exists and carry the day. This may well be rooted in Western philosophy and theology, in which speculative "proofs" of God's existence are advanced in the interest of establishing a first cause that serves as a cornerstone for proposed metaphysical systems. But we also need look no further than this tradition to gain insight into why proving God's existence is inherently problematic.

Perhaps the most widely invoked rationale for God, first proposed by the medieval scholar Ibn Sina (Avicenna), goes something like this: ***There must be a source or cause of our existence that, unlike our existence, is not contingent on something else.*** Otherwise we would have an endless chain of contingency. That first cause, with no other cause than itself, is God.

If one accepts this simple and apparently straightforward rationale for God's necessity, then God must be. God becomes metaphysically axiomatic so to speak, an acknowledged premise and self-evident truth. That this rationale is not tantamount to the incontrovertible proof of God's existence some have claimed or sought was hardly lost on Spinoza, Leibniz, and others who nevertheless embraced such a position. Nor did they dispute allegations of unsubstantiated assumptions and circular reasoning leveled by critics against this and other versions of the argument, most notably those put forward by Anselm and Descartes. That is the consequence of undertaking an exercise that cannot ultimately deliver on purely rational grounds because God by His very nature transcends our experience and understanding.

Indeed while no one has succeeded in crafting an airtight case for God's existence, more than a few have very clearly demonstrated why the expectation of proving (or disproving) God's existence cannot be met.

As philosopher and mathematician Bertrand Russell maintained, the only way to establish the existence of something is to demonstrate actual instances of it in the world. No amount of investigation of the *idea* that something exists can establish with certainty the *actual existence* of any instances of it. Since the Creator of the world is not *of* this world, and His transcendent Oneness further precludes any particular instances of his being in it, His actual existence, by this line of reasoning, can never be established.

Put another way, the statement "God exists," as Hume stipulated, is a statement of fact. Statements of fact are empirical statements that can be arrived at and validated only through sense experience, and cannot be known "apriori," or independent of such experience. They express contingent truths that could conceivably be otherwise. To say "God exists" is thus akin to saying "God is white-bearded." As God is not accessible to us through sense experience, there can be no determination of the fact of either His white-beardedness or His existence. Both statements equally presume a determination of fact where none can pertain.

By contrast such statements as "God is immutable," "God is eternal," or "God is infinite" are statements of identity that are true by definition. They express not contingent but necessary truths. Kant dubbed such utterances in which the predicate is already contained in the subject "analytical statements." Like God Himself none of these essential attributes ascribed to Him is something we are capable of experiencing, whether predicated of God or anything else. Immutability, eternity, infinity, perfection, and so on — be they innate ideas or extrapolated concepts — cannot be apprehended or validated by experience.

Indeed for Kant statements about any subject that express necessary or essential truths *cannot* be about existence. To say "a triangle is three-sided" or "man is a sentient creature" is true by definition and tells us nothing about whether a triangle or man exists. Once we predicate "existence" or any attribute that is not necessarily contained in the subject, we are in the realm of contingent truths that can only be validated empirically.

As a rationale for God's existence the original argument that *there must be a source or cause of our existence that, unlike our existence, is not contingent on something else* is not unencumbered by such complications. If existence as we know it is contingent, then by what license do we posit on the one hand the existence of that which is *not* contingent, and on the other the necessity of that whose existence we would so maintain? The severance of contingency from existence is the flipside of the conflation of existence and necessity implicated by the preceding arguments. This rationale cleverly manages both at the same time. That neither the necessity of anything that exists nor the existence of anything necessary can be demonstrably or defensibly asserted, however, is something that no sleight of logic can overcome.

Given all of the above we might reasonably conclude at

the very least that a preponderance of evidence validating or invalidating God's existence sufficient to settle the disputation once and for all — or even win converts from the other side — is not forthcoming. We might go so far as to renounce the discourse in its present form as little more than a self-indulgent exercise in futility. After all, when discourse is deadlocked it ceases to be discourse. Entrenched positions and tired arguments inflame the opposition without advancing the discussion. The hope of a meaningful and constructive dialogue would be to narrow the rift, if not ultimately close it. But that hope seems as naïve as it is remote. The one side will never prove that God exists any more than the other will prove that He does not. Neither is giving an inch, and never the twain shall meet.

But to leave it at that is to leave a genie with the power to change everything in the bottle. Suppose the apparent contradiction embedded in the ontological argument is pointing us to a truth that has not been adequately considered and whose importance has been vastly underestimated. If necessity and existence are mutually exclusive not just logically but *onto*logically, could something like a first cause then be ontologically *necessary* — meaning it must be — and *not* strictly speaking *exist*?

It sounds so preposterous that the mere suggestion is vexing. There is certainly no room in our understanding of reality for a God that is necessary but does not exist. In what kind of reality could such a profoundly counterintuitive notion make any sense at all, and what does it have to do with the one we live in?

The first part of this exploration addresses precisely this question. The premise and the terms on which the debate over God's existence has been conducted arise from an understanding of the world that you will be challenged to rethink in the pages ahead. We shall begin by marrying insights from philosophy and physics to draw some stunning if unabashedly speculative inferences that turn our notion of reality on its ear and lay the groundwork for a transformative new context in which traditional metaphysical and theological issues — including but not limited to the question of God's existence — might be re-evaluated and reconsidered.

You will be provoked throughout this investigation to let go of some widely held and deeply rooted conceptions about reality, God, and truth. You will be prompted to open your mind about God's identity and the role He plays in the world and in our lives. In the end — whichever side of the rift you now stand on and however deeply you have dug in your heels — you just might be compelled to change it.

Our journey is barely under way and already its rigors have begun to test us. That is as it should be; no expedition into uncharted territory is without its pitfalls. So let us forge ahead undaunted. A reality unfathomably strange yet inseparable from our own invites us to explore it.

I.

"Nothing is more abstract than reality."

— GIORGIO MORANDI

REALITY

Aptaeon
You maintain, revered Teacher, that the relative is determinate and the absolute indeterminate. Yet still my intuition resists this understanding.

Sagacites
It is indeed a perplexing notion, young Aptaeon.

Aptaeon
Surely we can ascribe to the absolute infinite rather than arbitrary exactitude, and so an absolute determinacy of which the relative is a mere approximation.

Sagacites
Perhaps together we can see our way clear of this misconception. Allow me to pose a simple question: Where are you?

Aptaeon

I am upon this bench beside you, revered Teacher, under this noble hemlock tree where daily we conduct our discourse.

Sagacites

I grant you that it is precisely so. And is not this description you give of your whereabouts in every respect relative?

Aptaeon

To this bench; to you; to the tree that gives us shade. Yes, it is.

Sagacites

Can you not answer the question without reference to any other object?

Aptaeon

I regret that I am unequipped to submit my exact latitude and longitude.

Sagacites

Relative to the equator and prime meridian…

Aptaeon

And therefore like my original response not absolute!

Sagacites

Now, once again, where are you?

Aptaeon *(flustered)*

I am… I am *here*, revered Teacher.

Sagacites

A most astute answer, young Aptaeon! Now cross this path and stand by the fence over there. *(Aptaeon complies.)* Where are you?

Aptaeon *(grinning broadly)*

I am *here*!

Sagacites

You are certain?

Aptaeon
Absolutely.

Sagacites beckons Aptaeon back to the bench.

Sagacites
There is no other statement of your position that does not invoke relativity?

Aptaeon
None.

Sagacites
So what have we learned?

Aptaeon
That absolute position is precisely and invariably here and here alone, revered Teacher.

Sagacites
And *when* are you here?

Aptaeon begins to reach for his pocket watch but stops himself.

Aptaeon *(confidently)*
I am here *now.*

Sagacites
You are sure you do not wish to consult your timepiece.

Aptaeon
And tell you when I am here according to the relative motion of the earth to the sun? I am quite sure.

Sagacites
Bravo. So what have we learned?

Aptaeon
That absolute time is precisely and invariably now and now alone.

Sagacites

And may we not refer to that absolute "herenowness" of which we speak as "presence" that transcends relativity and thereby determinacy?

Aptaeon

Yes, I should think so.

Sagacites

Now just to be sure no confusion remains — when you declared that you were here now, were you not in fact at two different places at two different times?

Aptaeon

First on this bench and then at that fence... This is true.

Sagacites

Yet you asserted your unchanging presence with equal conviction regardless of when and where you did so.

Aptaeon

I did.

Sagacites

So may we not say, young Aptaeon, that a thing's abiding presence in its essential absolutivity owes no allegiance whatsoever to any determinacy in space and time despite our expectations to the contrary?

Aptaeon

Truly, revered Teacher, it cannot be otherwise!

LIFTING THE VEIL OF DETERMINACY

IMAGINE STANDING BEFORE A SEURAT PAINTING. Natty Parisians enjoy an afternoon stroll. A tree shows off its lavish spring foliage. From a distance the shapes and hues appear definite and unambiguous. But as you draw closer to the canvas, all of that begins to change. What were moments ago clearly discernible tones and outlines are now indistinct and amorphous. The artwork has relinquished the sure and sensible forms you observed as you entered the gallery to reveal a fundamentally erratic and indefinite composition.

This may be the ultimate validation that life — or that which makes it possible — imitates art. Scientists who investigate the fundamental nature of reality are unmasking a world that on closer and closer inspection looks more like a Jackson Pollock than a Jan Vermeer, despite everything our experience tells us. In that world states of being and physical properties that we regard as mutually exclusive are impossibly wedded. It is as if an umbrella were at once open and closed, drying on the carpet even as it hangs from the coat rack above. Computers being modeled by quantum engineers won't use typical zero-or-one binary processing because the same "qubit" of information can be both a zero and a one!

Breathtaking strides made in quantum physics in the

past century have revealed the strange behavior of the stuff that lurks beneath our everyday reality and flies in the face of how we perceive, experience, and make sense of the world.

PURSUING THE THING-IN-ITSELF

The notion of a dichotomy between our experience of the world and an underlying reality hidden from us predates quantum physics. Since ancient times philosophers distinguished between the phenomenal appearance or sensible manifestations of objects and the actual objects of inquiry themselves.

Plato's inspired metaphor of the cave characterizes things as we perceive them as shadowy and imperfect semblances of numinous "Forms" that inhabit a loftier realm accessible to worldly aspirants only through that highest of faculties, reason. Centuries later George Berkeley asserted that there can be no matter without mind because its perceived qualities are entirely dependent on such observing minds, allowing for relative but not absolute perception, and Immanuel Kant concluded that any knowledge of a "transcendental object" existing independently of the observer is ultimately beyond our grasp. Because we rely entirely on categories of understanding inherent to our cognition like space and time to order and define experience, it is pointless even to consider the "thing-in-itself" outside the parameters of sensible intuition. For all we know — and will ever know — it is nothing more than an otherwise meaningless construct of our understanding. Where Plato found an avenue to virtuous enlightenment, Kant encountered a roadblock that knowledge cannot pass.

Undeterred by Kant's admonition of futility, scientists pursuing the thing-in-itself have devised clever experiments circumventing sensible intuition with very bizarre results. For example, when a light source is aimed at a plate with two slits for the light to pass through, photons striking a screen behind produce an interference pattern of bright and dark bands, consistent with a wave passing through both slits. (The same result has been reported with even a single photon!) But when a detector is placed at either slit to determine through which one a photon passes, the interference pattern on the screen disappears and the beam of light leaves the two distinct bands one would expect from a stream of discrete particles passing through one slit or the other.

It's as if the object under scrutiny divulges no specific, determinate position **unless** and **until** detected, and the act of observation disturbs or alters not just the results of the experiment but the nature of the object itself. True to the dichotomy established by philosophers, a difference is revealed in the nature of the object before and after it interacts with our environment and becomes fodder for our experience, or between the transcendental object and the "empirical object."

There is anything but consensus as to what all of this means. Is the indeterminate nature indicated of unobserved being **at all** real, **as** real as, or **more** real than the determinate character we observe? Does one really change into the other due to our intervention? Or does it merely **appear** to change with the two continuing to "coexist" on some level? Are we just chasing phantoms by drawing any metaphysical inferences whatsoever about these obliquely glimpsed but patently outlandish quantum behaviors? Is it enough simply to acknowledge such aberrations and accept the mathematical formalism that best describes them as the last word and the whole story?

THE THRESHOLD OF EMERGENCE

We shall not wait for consensus. We shall begin our own investigation right here, straddling the "threshold of emergence" between the transcendental and the empirical object, corresponding to the indeterminate and determinate states of being revealed before and after detection. We shall assume, as physicists increasingly concur, that what quantum theory is describing is real, and that it is moreover opening a window on the reality underlying our own, which would suggest not just a statistical but an ontic significance to these uncanny quantum rituals as well as their mathematical representations (which we shall leave to the mathematicians).

Let us start by comparing the object as unobserved and observed, and examining how the two relate to each other.

As unobserved the object's behavior is not what we would expect from a discrete particle with a definite position at any given time and a consequently predictable path. The quantum mechanical explanation points to an indefinite ensemble state of "superposition" in which no particular position among all of those possible is assumed and thus no single path taken to the exclusion of any other. As observed, on the other hand, the object takes on the particular definitive state that yields the determinate values we know and love. Scientists interpret this transition of states or phases as a "collapse" of the quantum superposition that occurs when the unobserved object interacts with the environment.

Some adhere to the notion of "decoherence," in which the interaction creates merely the *appearance* of collapse, such that the superposition remains but simply eludes measurement or determination in the context of our environment and experience. Proponents of this interpretation have also conjectured alternative histories (and worlds) in which collapse yields other possible states encompassed by the original ensemble state. While not without detractors, both ideas will play a prominent role going forward.

For now they will help us to establish and understand the relative ontological status of the empirical and transcendental object.

WHO'S ON FIRST?

How can we be sure that the unobserved, or transcendental, object is prior and fundamental to the observed, or empirical, object and the latter contingent on the former? Why couldn't the reverse be true, or the two possess ontological parity?

The conjectured collapse of the ensemble state of the unobserved object into the singular state of the observed object implies not just a state change but also a direction of change from the ensemble to the singular state. It could not be otherwise because the ensemble state includes all possible singular states that the particle might acquire. Its determinate properties, in other words, cannot fall outside the parameters allowed by the ensemble state. Any particular position or spin or other property ultimately assumed by the empirical object — even if specifically dictated by other, perhaps random, influences — is nevertheless delineated by and thus contingent upon the transcendental object.

That the collapse only *appears* to mutate the transcendental object does not invalidate this relationship. There is nevertheless a *translation*, which is also an abridgment, *from* the complex ensemble state of the transcendental object *to* the simple definitive state of the empirical object. In the reduction from unabridged to abridged version, all information beyond the determinacies assumed by the empirical object is edited out and *effectively* lost because it cannot be assimilated by the empirical object or accommodated by its environment. Since that information remains unavailable, it cannot be regained to make the translation back to the unabridged version.

It is more accurate to think of the translation as "unidirectional" rather than "irreversible" because, to the extent that the reduction emerges only in the context of the empirical environment, there is really nothing to reverse: the superposition is transcendentally intact and the transcendental object itself unaffected. (This interpretation is supported by findings that when information is detected and then quickly "erased" before the particle hits the screen, it leaves an interference pattern reflecting the superposition, despite the earlier detection.)

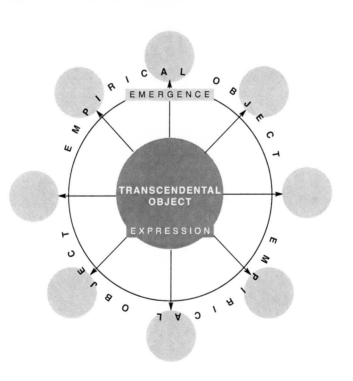

The one-way direction of translation indicates not just the contingency of the empirical on the transcendental object but the *emergence* of the one from the other by means of a reduction from the unabridged to abridged state of being such that the empirical object is just one possible expression — and therefore a limited and qualified one — of the transcendental object. The particular expression that emerges in our environment is not exclusive insofar as other reductions may yield other determinacies with alternative histories in parallel environments. In that case expression by the transcendental object is not singular and linear but manifold and "radiant," such that any number of determinate reductions emanate at once, although with only one observable outcome per environment.

Our experiment is showing us just one spoke of the wheel.

THE MOON IS REALLY THERE

We have seen that when we avert our gaze the thing under scrutiny ceases to manifest the guise it presents to us. Conversely, when we direct our attention to something it appears to disturb or alter that thing in no small way. Thus we may draw the conclusion per Berkeley's philosophy of immaterialism that the thing as we experience it exists only in the context of experience. It sounds like a clear enough statement, but it is all too easy to misinterpret.

Picture yourself taking a midnight stroll on the beach under a full moon. No one is there but you. All is quiet save for the surf breaking gently at your feet. Does your sensible intuition and consciousness of the moon somehow conjure it into existence? When you turn away does it in any sense at all cease to exist? Not as long as it bathes you in its light, commands the tides, and inspires lovers to romance! You and the moon and everything else in the universe are in this together.

In other words, even if detection or observation of the object and any given property under consideration is "coercive" and precipitates the reduction into the specific determinate value measured (at least on the micro level of un-aggregated subatomic particles), it does not follow that we are conjuring or controlling that reality with our conscious minds, as our observation does not in and of itself dictate *which* reduction actualizes, except to the extent that we contribute to the overall existential-empirical context into which it emerges.

Rather experience and existence must be viewed as flip-sides of the same ontological context. If there is no existence outside the realm of experience, then there is equally no experience outside the realm of existence. Consider the proverbial poser *If a tree falls in the forest and no one is there to hear it does it make a sound?* Should we not ask for that matter whether absent the observer it even falls in the first place, or going further still, whether the tree is really there to begin with at all? While we may not be within our ratiocinative rights to disjoin the sound of the tree falling from the hearing of it, if it *does* fall and you *are* there, then you had better get out of the way. It is spurious to conclude that existence is unilaterally contingent on experience, much less on an individual's subjective experience, relativity notwithstanding.

The truth, however, may turn out to be even more radical than the misinterpretation. Both existence and experience are equally contingent on something transcendent and imperceptible. That is exactly what we are glimpsing when the particle reveals its hidden face. The particle is the existential expression of that transcendental object, which is neither accessible to our intuition nor accounted for by our categories of understanding.

And that is precisely why we need to change them.

LET'S GET METAPHYSICAL

We must account in the model of reality postulated here for two "modalities" of being: 1) the emergent or conditional modality of the empirical object, and 2) the pre-emergent or unconditional modality of the transcendental object that expresses it.

Insofar as the former manifests the determinate properties that define our existence and delimit our experience, we shall refer to it as *existential* or, alternatively, *emergent being*. Insofar as the latter encompasses all possible determinacies that it may express in any emergent reduction, and is thus necessary for and inherent to its existence, we shall refer to it as *essential being*. We may also refer to it as *fundamental* or *transcendental* being.

ESSENCE		EXISTENCE
expressive		emergent
transcendental		empirical
indeterminate superposition		determinate reduction
necessary	THRESHOLD OF EMERGENCE	contingent
absolute		qualified
potential		actual

Thus we have *essential being* on one side of the threshold of emergence and *existential being* on the other. This interpretation of the dichotomy between the transcendental object, or thing-in-itself, and the empirical object, or its observable manifestation(s), will serve us for the remainder of this exploration.

The thing-in-itself, while typically associated with actuality in much the way you might regard it as the "actual" thing, is identified here instead with potentiality in encompassing the possibilities for existence. As only the phenomenal manifestations expressed by it *actualize*, so too only those substantially downgraded expressions of the thing-in-itself may be allied with actuality. In this we follow more closely in the metaphysical footsteps of Plato than Aristotle, and echo Neoplatonists like Plotinus.

"WRONG-WAY" REDUCTION
AND ITS IMPLICATIONS

Implicit in the ontological dichotomy we have just drawn is an epistemological twist that demands our attention before we proceed. The pursuit of anything fundamental is generally thought of as a reductionist exercise that takes us from something derivative and relatively complex to something formative and relatively simple; the analysis gets increasingly granular until we arrive at that which is ultimately irreducible. One might expect the quest for fundamental being to be no different, nor indeed has it been with the discovery of molecules and atoms and subatomic particles.

But here that expectation has already been confounded. Why? Because it is *not* the primary modality of essential being that is a reduction of the derivative modality of existential being, but the other way around. As expressed in our environment, the complex and unabridged essential state of being reduces to the single definite state experienced, observed, and measured by us. Thus the reduction from complexity to simplicity occurs not in the direction *toward* fundamentality but *away* from it.

But if we are to assert that essential being is irreducible, how can there be any reduction of it at all? There is a reduction vis-à-vis any given environment in which a particular determinate outcome actualizes, though *not* across all environments. The unabridged state remains essentially intact and inviolable, moreover, so the overlying abridgment can hardly be considered a component or constituent (as an atom is of a molecule) from which the original complex state

28

is aggregated. It is rather a particular (and particulate) expression. Such a reduction has no place in the hierarchy of complexity that we ascribe to actualized emergent systems.

This "wrong-way reduction" is striking nevertheless because it is both counterintuitive and disorienting to find our own reality and modality of being to be a reduction in any sense of that from which it emerges (although the shadows on the wall of Plato's cave arguably make a similar point), and to find our quest for what is essential and primordial beckoning us toward complexity rather than the simplicity and granularity we seek.

We must brace ourselves for the possibility that fundamental being may resist the kind of reducibility that gives us answers of simple and ordered "elegance" sought and favored by scientists and mathematicians. In his own "meta-mathematical" investigations, Gregory Chaitin argues to the contrary that we may ultimately find in our quest for truth, as he has, infinite complexity. Among real numbers after all, the *rationals* (expressed as ratios of whole numbers, fractions, or decimals with finite places) that we use in our everyday lives — as well as for scientific measurements and computations because they allow us to arrive at precisely determinate and computable values — are vastly outnumbered by *irrationals* (expressed as decimals that go on forever), which defy infinitely precise evaluation and pose serious computational challenges. Most of these are *transcendental numbers* like π that cannot even be expressed algebraically, making matters still more difficult. Of these, a portion could never be generated given all the time in the world because their random sequence of digits precludes the possibility of any algorithm capable of enumerating them. Chaitin's constant, or Ω, a real number (or actually multiple numbers) identified by Chaitin as a result of his work in number theory, falls into this final category, and he believes that its infinite, indefinite, and incomputable character may very well reflect the ultimate nature of reality. The conclusion — albeit meta-mathematically rather than meta-physically drawn — that radical complexity and indeterminacy are archetypal and fundamental notably parallels the position arrived at here.

Finally, we must also recognize the analytical challenge of making sense of a prior mode of being that is by its nature unintelligible. Kant posited the transcendental object as beyond our apprehension and comprehension, and the indirect glimpses that we have nevertheless managed of it ironically end up supporting his contention. Indeed, now we can be even more forthright. Our sensory-cognitive apparatus simply does not have the resolving power or bandwidth to process more complex superposed or ensemble states of being. Essential reality is full-def and our cognitive apparatus is constructed within and in order to interpret a relatively low-def existential environment!

OBVENTS AND TRANJECTS

While our discussion so far of emergent being has referred to the "object" of experience, this is somewhat misleading as the word "object" captures only the spatial character of that entity. Every existential object is equally an "event" with determinate temporal as well as spatial properties. These can no more be divorced from one another than can space from time. Existential being is defined by its temporality. Characterized by inevitable and irrevocable change, its being is becoming. Thus discrete existential entities are more accurately thought of as object-events, or "obvents." They cannot emerge with exclusively spatial or temporal properties but always manifest both.

What about the transcendental object, hereafter "tranject," of essential being? How does something that does not even possess a definite state of being undergo change? If it is neither this nor that, it cannot change from this *to* that. If it is neither here nor there, it cannot go from here *to* there. In its expression of the obvent, the reduction is an observed or experienced phenomenon and not an inherent one, meaning its original complex state is essentially retained. In other words, the tranject never "commits" to particular states or properties outside its existential expression. It remains in and of itself *un*changed. Essential being is thus being *without* becoming. Because it expresses at once all the possibilities of its being, it cannot become anything that it is not already, and it cannot be otherwise. It is thus not temporal in nature, but eternal.

This is meant not in the sense of everlasting or enduring throughout time, but apart from time. Indeed, physicists have surmised that space and time themselves may be emergent phenomena not fundamentally inherent to being. In Kantian terms space and time are categories of understanding by which we intuit the sensible object. As features of experience they lay no claim whatever to the transcendental object. By that line of reasoning essential being transcends space and time along with experience. Trying to conceive of anything before it or after it, beyond it or outside it is senseless. This is entirely consistent with the view hinted at earlier that the tranject has a presence independent of the existential-empirical context.

To summarize, obvents , or *existentia,* are phenomenal expressions of tranjects, or *essentia,* that actualize with determinate properties in a spacetime environment formed and fashioned as a "byproduct" of their emergence. (Spacetime is delineated and demarcated only by what occurs within it.) The tranjects that express such obvents are themselves unaltered by expression and retain their complex timeless and immutable nature, which eludes determinacy. So the transcendental "object" originally sought by this inquiry has turned out to be something of a contradiction in terms because the spatial and temporal particularity that give the obvent its object-like character is precisely what essential being transcends.

THIS MAGIC MOMENT

We have characterized existential being as obvents defined as much by their temporal as by their spatial properties. Despite our tendency to sunder time and space into distinct concepts, the interplay is reflected in our everyday language with expressions like "events take place" or "things happen." But perhaps only when we talk about something being "present" does a single word evoke both space and time.

While time and space may be inextricable, understanding the existence of things in time poses by far the thornier challenge. After all, we can see in both directions and stop or reverse direction in any of the three spatial dimensions. But in the one temporal dimension we can neither stop nor reverse direction, nor even see in the direction we are headed. And there's that irksome way that time has of slipping through our fingers and resisting any attempt to hold on to it. That makes it tough to wrap our heads around even the basic identity of something that is subject to and undergoes constant change. Am I the same person I was a moment ago and will be a moment from now? Do I even exist in any other moment than this one in which I am now present?

Two schools of thought have emerged in response to such questions. One holds that an individual entity is wholly present at every moment of its existence and thereby sustains an enduring identity. The other maintains that an entity is composed of various temporal parts extending across spacetime, or that an entity identified with a particular temporal part exists only for an instant but by virtue of parts related in some way exists in successive "stages" through which its identity is sustained.

Let's invoke a familiar analogy to help us think about our existence and identity in time. Imagine a film that's all about you. Each frame of the film is a moment in your life and the sum of frames your lifetime. While you appear throughout the film, you are present only at that moment when the film passes behind the lens of the projector. That's the moment you (and the audience) experience as now. Both schools of thought borrow to some degree from the film analogy the idea that you exist frame-to-frame or moment-to-moment, with your identity somehow sustained from one to the next. Yet our understanding of existential being as becoming would suggest otherwise. The persistence of your identity in time cannot be considered an element separate from your existence that binds it together like some kind of temporal glue. It is rather precisely what defines your existence. Your existence is established not by the isolated frames of film but by the film's continuity. Your presence in the here and now, or in the frame projected on the screen, is exceptional because only in the moment do you transcend your fleeting existence. When we speak of "living in the moment" or "seizing the moment," we articulate this very sense of engagement by our temporal being with a timeless now.

It may feel as if we are in the moment and then the moment passes. But it's not the moment that passes. It's the *we*. Just as the film rolls by the fixed window behind the lens on the projector, our temporal being continually recedes from the present. That's the defining feature of existence and the existential condition.

We are ultimately misled by the film analogy when we think of our existence in time as a succession of frames or moments. There is nothing of a momentary nature about temporal existence except where it meets the present. When we refer to past or future moments, it is solely in recollection or anticipation of experiencing them as now. What's more, to regard a span of time as successive moments creates the problem of having to assign to those moments some absolute duration that would be impossible to determine even if there were one. But just as a point has no extension in space, the moment has no duration in time. We are present in the moment because only in the moment does existence admit emergence and becoming yield to being.

If we look to establish persistence of identity as presence throughout temporal existence, then we fail to acknowledge the timeless nature of the present. Presence *does not* persist. If we seek existence in instants or increments of time, we wrest existence from temporality and face the problem of having to assign to those instants of existence durations that do not pertain. Existence *is* persistence.

No sooner does existential being emerge than it assumes an intrinsically temporal identity. How it retains its identity through the changes it undergoes as temporal being is a question that arises when we view time as a succession of present moments. That's a mistake. The present moment is not a piece of time but the junction of time and timelessness. And our presence in the moment is our window on eternity in the dark fortress of our temporal existence.

PRESENT AND ANTECEDENT CAUSALITY

Because an obvent expresses with duration, or extension in time, as well as in space, it is itself a spacetime continuum along which outcomes emerge and constitute its being as becoming. Its existence may be understood precisely as spacetime extension, or the sum of outcomes spanning the entirety of its becoming. Through our sensible intuition of the obvent we experience these outcomes successively, apprehending an entity actualized in time that appears to be fully expressed and to which change appears to be subsequent or secondary to being already established. What we are witnessing in such change, however, is nothing other than the partial expression of the obvent as effected by constituent outcomes produced through two kinds of causality: *present* and *antecedent.*

The presence of an obvent is established directly with no prior or intermediate contingency from the tranject that expresses it. Essential being is thus the present cause of every obvent and emergent outcome that constitutes and defines it. Insofar as the obvent is a direct and immediate expression of essential being, its presence is timeless and cannot be construed in that capacity as the effect or result of any prevailing conditions or circumstances.

The existential identity and composition of an obvent, at the same time, is radically contingent upon prevailing conditions and circumstances, including its own pre-existing identity, within an actualized environment. All prior outcomes and interacting obvents that have participated in its becoming are its antecedent causes. They comprise the complex chain of cascading contingency and causality that we associate with our existence.

Present causality produces *immediate* outcomes. Antecedent causality produces *mediate* outcomes, or consequences. This is an important distinction. Your existential identity is a consequence of your parents meeting and giving birth to and raising you, and the sum of all of your experiences and interactions to date. Your presence in the world as your parents' child and a college graduate and a dog lover and everything else is an immediate outcome of your essential being (notwithstanding your complexity relative to the isolated particle first considered). While antecedent causes influence and direct emergent outcomes, such outcomes must ultimately issue from a present cause, as a direct expression of essential being.

Thus every mediate outcome that transfigures entity and actuality alike is attendant to an immediate outcome (or aggregate of outcomes), which is a partial expression of essential being as abridged by the existential context. The *transference* of cause and effect from and to the environment by which antecedent causality acts on the entity is not sufficient to impart the ontic integrity, immediacy, and substantiality that come only through *emergence* via present causality. Without it we would be left with all of the frailty of becoming and none of the firmity of being.

This hardly dilutes the determinism of antecedent causality. Whereas essential being as a present cause effects all possible outcomes that may determine a particular obvent, not all such outcomes are admissible in a given actualized environment. For one thing, outcomes that are mutually exclusive existentially cannot emerge together, as an obvent cannot be in two places or states at the same time. For another, certain possible outcomes may be inadmissible as eventualities due to restrictions imposed by the prevailing actuality. If you had picked your beloved pooch from a litter of purebred Cocker Spaniels, you would be unlikely to come home this evening to a drooling Rottweiler. By prompting, directing, and filtering outcomes admissible within and by virtue of the prevailing actuality (by means of natural selection, one might say) antecedent causes forge the existential identity of the obvent.

Present causality is not easily grasped in classical terms. The present cause may be thought of as a *first cause*, as there is nothing in turn that causes it, though not in the sense of an initial cause or first step in the sequential chain of cause and effect that unfolds over time. By the same token it may not be regarded as a *final cause* in which the ultimate purpose or culmination of a thing's development is encoded, as that notion is likewise confined to its becoming. Nor may it be considered a *material cause* of which the end product physically consists: The present cause expresses materially but has itself no material properties. It could be considered a *formal cause* inasmuch as it contains the prior essential capacity (if not a literal "blueprint") for a thing to exist. It might further be seen as an *efficient cause* that brings about a possible result without necessitating a particular result, but never as a consequence of any interactivity in space and time. That is the domain of antecedent causality. From present causality issues only the timeless presence of each obvent, and not any contingency, continuity, or causality established in the actualized environment.

UNIVERSE, MULTIVERSE, PRIMAVERSE

Let us return to the threshold of emergence between essential and existential being. Looking one way we see the timeless indeterminacy of an eternal present. Looking the other we see determinate obvents arise, evolve, and perish. Looking one way we see essential being embrace the bountiful possibilities of creation. Looking the other we see existential being actualize with particular expression in a discernible progression.

From here it is apparent that any such chronology or history of determinate outcomes (beginning with the inception of the universe) is an exclusively emergent phenomenon. It does not pertain essentially because the indeterminacy of essential being is not expended or ceded in its expression of emergent outcomes. Those obvents actualize only existentially; nothing "happens" and there are no consequences except in that context and environment. Being never lapses into becoming. Present never slips into past. No chronology or history is established. Nothing is irrevocable because all possible outcomes remain eternally so. That regrettable spending spree you succumbed to last weekend is no more set in stone than the tentative lunch scheduled with your client next Tuesday!

Any history of determinate events is also, moreover, local to a particular universe. Essential being is not confined in its expression to the eventualities that make up our timeline and universe. Mutually exclusive or environmentally inadmissible outcomes may emerge in "parallel" or "alternate" universes. Thus every point of emergence is equally a point of divergence at which alternative outcomes actualize in and establish another environment. This is consistent with the "Many Worlds Interpretation" conjectured by physicists, or a *multiverse*, in which our universe is but one of a great — perhaps infinite — number.

Our universe thus represents but one particular space-time scenario, which emerges and unfolds in one of countless possible ways. That means the universe is hardly that single all-encompassing domain we once imagined it to be. Not even the multiverse, for that matter, can contain the essential being of which it is the rich and varied expression.

It may therefore be constructive to postulate a *primaverse* in which essential being "resides." This gives us the semantic freedom and conceptual license to trespass into that forbidden realm independent of space and time and experience out of which emergent being arises. We'll stay out of trouble as long as we leave our space probes and spectrometers behind with the understanding that "exploring the primaverse" is a metaphor for the purposes of a purely metaphysical exercise.

A visual analogy might help us get a better handle on the foregoing discussion. Imagine a sphere covered with points connected by line segments like the one in the illustration. Starting at the "north pole" we may trace a pathway southward by choosing a line segment emanating from each point. This is your universal timeline. At each point of emergence (and divergence) more than one outcome is available but only one can actualize. There are plenty of alternate pathways we could have drawn on the surface of the sphere from the same starting point. Taken together, these constitute the multiverse.

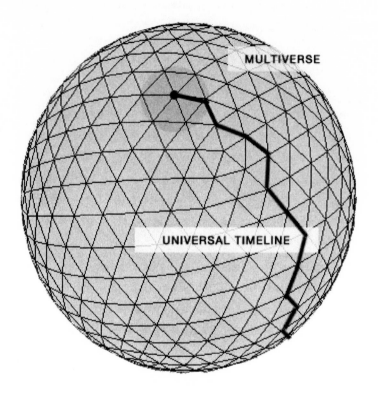

The analogy is crude but illustrative. As obvents actualize in universal spacetime, available outcomes are directed and limited by the prevailing actuality, or what has already happened. This creates the cascading causality we experience from one outcome to the next as our universal or personal history unfolds.

Now let's go inside the sphere to the central point at its core. Imagine lines radiating from that point to every point on the surface — where the line segments intersect as well as the segments themselves. Think of these lines radiating from the core as eternally "active," animating all the points and all the possible pathways between them. This is the primaverse.

Primaversally, all admissible outcomes are equally and timelessly viable. Because spacetime is indelible immanently but not transcendentally, no possible expression of essential being is ever suppressed or excluded except within the actualized environment. There is only present causality, direct and unmediated from essential to emergent being. No point of emergence (not even the first) has priority or precedence over another, and no point or pathway is exclusive to any other.

In short, every possible outcome encompassed essentially expresses existentially, even if our experience is limited to one particular outcome at any point in spacetime and one succession of outcomes across spacetime. From the primaverse emanates not just our world, but all possible worlds.

EXPRESSION AS FULFILLMENT
AND THE REASON FOR EXISTENCE

If essential being is by its nature inherently expressive, then its expressive activity and behavior is not incidental but necessary as an integral part of its broader ontological necessity. This is implicit in the contention that every possible expression of essential being emerges, even though it may never actualize in our environment or experience.

There is no contradiction whatsoever between this necessity of *expression* and the contingency of *what is expressed* particularly because it does not follow from the contingency of emergent, or expressed, entities that expression is itself contingent, or unnecessary. Moreover, that the necessity of expression cannot be extricated from that of essential being gives us an unambiguous reason for existence, or why there is something rather than nothing. Very simply, essential being must — and therefore does — express, in the form of emergent being.

As a necessary and inherent behavior of essential being, expression further represents a "fulfillment" of its nature. But we must be careful not to interpret such fulfillment as having a beneficial or sustaining "effect" on essential being, which is absolute and immutable and thus cannot undergo change. To the extent that essential being is eternal and its expressions primaversally timeless, it is never *un*fulfilled. Thus fulfillment is not a consequence of expression, nor expression a cause of fulfillment. Rather both expression *and* fulfillment are mutually and eternally realized.

WRAPPING OUR HEADS AROUND TRANJECTS

If obvents are the stuff of the universe (and multiverse), then tranjects are the stuff of the primaverse — the irreducible, imperishable, and eternal constituents of being. We have proposed that unlike obvents, which emerge as actualized existentia with determinate spacetime extension, tranjects retain their spacetime-transcendent, unabridged, and indeterminate complexity. As such, tranjects do not possess the matter and form that make obvents intelligible. They operate on a scale small enough to express a single electron and vast enough to express an entire universe. They are fundamental and formative, germinal and incipient, yet hardly simple or tangible.

How do we even begin to make heads or tails of that?

Since we are obviously way out of our cognitive comfort zone here, we must take pains not to draw inferences based on experience or draw parallels or correspondences between obvents and tranects that do not pertain. The temptation is to envisage these tranjects as analogous but pre-emergent entities that correspond to or organize along the lines of the obvents they express. Is this making unwarranted inferences right out of the gate?

At the risk of taking a depressing turn, imagine a universe in which your life tragically ends in childhood, and another in which your parents never meet and thus you are not born at all. The tranjects that express your existence do not perish with you in the first instance, nor are they absent in the second. As these scenarios illustrate, neither the features nor even the very fact of your existence similarly limit or qualify the essential being that expresses them. The tranjects are present whether or not you are, so we cannot infer some exclusive and proprietary bundle of essential being that individuates as you do.

The explanation for this goes back to spacetime determinacy. What differentiates you as an individual in both physicality and consciousness, and distinguishes you from any other obvent, is your unique and determinate trajectory in spacetime. Consider identical twins. They're made from the same genetic information (and one might infer the same essential being), yet they are separate individuals. That's *only* because they have different spacetime extensions. Solely by virtue of such spacetime extensions are their distinct and divergent identities forged and shaped by antecedent causality, or the interactions among obvents in the actualized environment.

As all of this happens emergently, none of it pertains to essential being, which is spacetime-transcendent. All our nows are primaversally, or tranjectively, one now; all our heres, one here. With no spacetime extension, the distinctions we draw between physical or conscious identities do not apply, so tranjects cannot be individuated or differentiated in the way that we are, if at all. Furthermore, there is no internal causality primaversally; the chain of cause and effect kicks in post-emergently as well. Thus expression by essential being cannot be the result of additive interactions or "interdeterminism" among the tranjects; they cannot causally affect one another and must therefore be fully autonomous. If fully autonomous, they must be intrinsically equipped with everything they need in order to conduct their business of infinite and eternal expression.

TRANJECTIVE ABSOLUTIVITY
AND ESSENTIAL INTIMACY

If individuation or separability does not apply to tranjects as an inadmissible extrapolation from the object of experience, how can we even think in terms of a multiplicity (or infinity) of tranjects?

Spacetime determinacy sets up a relativity among obvents such that they are existentially defined and differentiated by their relation to and interaction with one another and the environment they comprise. The more proximate in space and time another obvent is to you, the greater its potential determinism on your own being; the more remote in space and time, the more negligible. The individuated identities and consequential differentiation of existentia are thus profoundly relative.

As spacetime transcendent, on the other hand, tranjects must be defined not relatively but absolutely. With no spacetime context, no tranject is more proximate to or remote from any other. With no consequent relativity, it is neither defined by its relation to other tranjects nor subject to extrinsic influences exerted by them. Because its identity is intrinsic and not forged by individuation, it is not itself individuated and thereby segregated from other tranjects. Absent such segregation, any notion of "multiplicity" characterized by strictly proprietary and discretely differentiated identities would not pertain.

Before we conclude that such tranjects must therefore be regarded not as many but as one, however, we must be equally wary of any unity that would preclude multiplicity. After all, if that which we identify as a single particle can experience interference (with itself) just as that which we identify as multiple particles can do, then surely we must dispense in this exotic realm with the distinctions we draw existentially between part and whole, selfsame and other, many and one.

spacetime determinacy	OBVENTIVE RELATIVITY	existential individuation
transcendental indeterminacy	TRANJECTIVE ABSOLUTIVITY	essential intimacy

Perhaps we can find an analogy in nature with corals or fungi that propagate vast colonies in which the identity of individuals and the whole blur into one. Perhaps we can find it with the neurons of the brain, which specialize in interpreting certain kinds of signals or generating certain kinds of impulses but also appear to have a general functionality that transcends any particular role. Are tranjects bound like neurons by a holistic "consciousness" that allows them to operate in concert, if not collaboratively? Is it Leibniz's perfect harmony, or Chaitin's random anarchy?

If all of this paints a picture (definitely a Jackson Pollock!) of essential being, it is one of independent yet indivisible entities united by purpose and identity, pure and autonomously expressive potentialities with absolute creative sovereignty.

Reality

Let us borrow (and perhaps take a few additional liberties with) the metaphor of "strings" invoked by theoretical physicists in the naming and explaining of string theory. As fundamental constituents of being, these strings express emergent states and properties by vibrating or resonating at particular frequencies. Viewed through the prism of this metaphysics, these strings do not essentially resonate at any one frequency to the exclusion of any other. Nor can any single string be isolated from the entire orchestra; there are no solo performances in the primaverse. All strings play eternally in concert one grand and spontaneous composition from which emanates all of creation.

Who but God could conduct such a divine symphony?

*"All things have sprung from nothing and are borne forward to infinity.
Who can follow out such an astonishing career?
The Author of these wonders, and He alone, can comprehend them."*

— BLAISE PASCAL

GOD

Sagacites

Good day, young Aptaeon. My eyesight has begun to fail me, but I am quite sure that I saw you leaving the temple not an hour ago.

Aptaeon

I stopped to say a prayer for my ailing grandmother. Yet no sooner had I knelt before the altar than I realized how foolish that would be.

Sagacites

How so?

Aptaeon

Surely her fate is already decided.

Sagacites

And you have resigned yourself to it?

Aptaeon

I have, revered Teacher. Our destiny is preordained by God and we are powerless to change it.

Sagacites

If our destiny were so preordained, then would not God, too, be powerless to change it?

Aptaeon

He wills it in the first place and in His infinite wisdom has no reason to change it.

Sagacites

Is not God's power like His wisdom infinite?

Aptaeon

That has always been my belief.

Sagacites

Yet you contend that had He the will to do so for whatever reason, He would be as powerless as you and I are to change what is to be.

Aptaeon

If our lot is predestined, then how can it be otherwise?

Sagacities

Is not God in His infinite presence *everywhen* as well as everywhere?

Aptaeon

It is undoubtedly the case.

Sagacites

And would not His supreme will then enjoy eternal free reign at every point in time whether by our reckoning past, present, or future?

Aptaeon

It would seem to follow.

Sagacites

Then at what point in time would He have fixed these particular outcomes so indelibly, and under what constraint would He be to do so?

Aptaeon

There would be no such point in time, and He would be under no such constraint.

Sagacites

Does not your view of predestination then belie the absolute and timeless nature of God's will?

Aptaeon

It does, revered Teacher. God's supreme will and providence do not fix indelibly what was, is, or will be!

Sagacites

May we not then invoke them whenever and wherever we may be present to whatever end we have set our hearts on that He Himself may entertain?

Aptaeon

We most assuredly may.

Sagacites

Perhaps your supplication on your grandmother's behalf is not so misguided after all.

Aptaeon

I shall pray for her this very night, and every other.

REVISITING THE ONTOLOGICAL ARGUMENT

WE HAVE CHARACTERIZED ESSENTIAL BEING as absolute, eternal, and immutable: attributes typically ascribed to divine being. By expressing the determinate outcomes that make up existential being, it is the progenitor of our world and all that arises within it. How can we help but see in this expressive nature of essential being — conscious, willful, or otherwise — the Hand of God? Is this not the cause with no other cause than itself?

As promised we now find ourselves back where we started, but we return with a dramatically different perspective. Let us now recall the quandary implicit in the ontological argument for God's necessity: If existence is inherently contingent — with no intrinsic necessity — then how can any first cause postulated break free of contingency without also casting off existence?

It cannot. And with the understanding of being proposed here the rationale presents no contradiction. Simply stated, God cannot be considered existential being. As essential being, He is indeed necessary but *does not exist*. The contradiction arises only when we would predicate of Him both necessity and existence, as that is a category mistake produced by conflating modalities of being. To require existence of God and seek determinate validation thereof is to regard Him as an actualized obvent, or expression of essential being, which is by definition a limited, finite, and temporal reduction of it. Only emergent being is characterized by the determinate spacetime extension necessary for sensible intuition and empirical determination. As eternally present, being without becoming, God's identity transcends not only experience but also existence (per Plotinus).

Anselm's argument to demonstrate God's existence is built on the premise that that which exists is "greater" than that which does not. As the greatest conceivable being, God must exist or else a being still greater could be conceived — one that *does* exist. We hereby refute the premise and thus the conclusion by maintaining that that which exists is rather a limited expression of that which is essential. After all, is not all that can be greater than that which happens to be; primaverse greater than universe; God greater than Creation?

To objectify or "existentialize" God is no less inappropriate than to anthropomorphize Him. Both extrapolate features of emergent being and impose on essential being qualifications that do not pertain.

One need not — and ought not — accept God's existence to acknowledge His necessity. God is not an existential being and therefore cannot be said to exist, only to "inhere" or "ensist," if you will. He is pure essence and pure presence, and the existence He expresses and suffuses does not delimit, diminish, or define Him, and so cannot be predicated of Him.

DISTINGUISHING GOD FROM CHARACTERIZATIONS OF GOD

Equating God with essential being or a metaphysical first cause is hardly the picture painted of Him in Sunday school, or the one most of us take to heart. Indeed, religions and religious sects sprout and splinter and wars are fought based on depictions of God, and people embrace or reject God accordingly.

Fortunately, this exploration does not require that we take sides. On the contrary, it requires that we do not. No description or characterization of God can adequately encompass Him as absolute and unqualified being because such descriptions and characterizations by definition qualify, and therefore none can truly and wholly represent or reveal God. It is a limitation not just of our language, but of the nature of our contingent and qualified being. As Wittgenstein — and before him Thomas Aquinas — noted, any talk of God must be by analogy.

This is not to dismiss any of these characterizations that serve the purpose of making God more accessible to us by giving Him features we might grasp and a face we might recognize. But it is crucial because it means that rejecting any or even *all* characterizations of God is not tantamount to rejecting God. Religion, while based on faith in God, has a monopoly neither on faith nor God because neither can be contained by any characterization of Him, or rituals of worship observed, or institutional dogma prescribed.

Even for self-professed, card-carrying atheists, it is not

so easy to renounce God! At the end of the day, the only legitimate grounds for rejecting God is to reject the necessity of a first and ultimate cause of contingent being, or the equivalence of that to God. Likewise, renouncing faith, and not just religion, would be to reject an absolute underpinning or unqualified truth that anchors contingent being. To say you have faith but not in God might be contradictory insofar as any principles, ideals, or truths embraced — despite examples one may cite empirically — transcend any possible and particular situation, and as such are arguably anchored in essential being, or God, in the pure form by which you set your moral or behavioral or even rational compass.

None of this is intended to convince anyone to accept rather than reject God. This is not an evangelistic undertaking. Rather, it is meant to frame the argument in the most fundamental and dispassionate terms we can establish, even if arbitrarily, for the purposes of traditional metaphysical inquiry, in which God is not at all inconspicuous. It thus paves the way for us to weigh in on some longstanding metaphysical issues as they relate to the notion of God.

IS GOD IMPOTENT?

The same allegation that was leveled against Aristotle that God cannot do anything that He is not already doing can be leveled here. The conclusion reached that this therefore makes Him powerless is easily refuted.

Power as we wield it and thus understand it is the ability to effect change and thereby produce "new" outcomes. As God is primaversal being, change is not in his wheelhouse. Instead, His creativity is eternal, which means all possible outcomes are eternally expressed. But it is existentially provincial to infer from this that He is "already" doing everything He can be and is consequently powerless because the notion of "already" has no valid content except in the context of our own limited existence.

Creation is a timeless work in progress and the outcomes never expended primaversally. That you dug up your strawberry patch and planted blueberries limits your next harvest to blueberries. For God your next harvest could be blueberries, raspberries, or gooseberries and, for that matter, so could your *last* harvest. So whose power is greater: yours to effect change within the constraints of everything that has happened before and is happening around you now, or His to reconceive and recreate all of it including you timelessly and unconditionally?

For God all of time is an open book and He does not write it in indelible ink. If He ceased His expression, then not only would nothing be, but nothing would ever have been. That God is doing everything He can be in no way

God

renders Him powerless. His omnipotence is absolute and unrestricted because the fulfillment and realization of His infinite expressiveness is eternal and inexhaustible.

EMERGENCE AND ALIENATION

To come into existence is to be profoundly alienated from our essential being.

With actualization emergent being undergoes a detachment from its own essence, or God. As it dons the mantle of determinacy, it is distanced from His omnipotence. As it assumes the mode of becoming, it is exiled from His eternal presence.

The sense of wanting and trepidation at the heart of existentialism is nothing other than a visceral awareness of the condition and limitations of our temporal being. That distress is equally a restless and insatiable yearning rooted in our own imperishable essence for communion, or reunion, with that which is primordial, eternal, and free of the shackles of determinacy. Emergent being is drawn to its essential nature, which is always present though shrouded in existence.

Thus we balance the despair of existential alienation with the desire for essential reconciliation, and strive for authenticity, fulfillment, enlightenment, salvation — in whatever guise and through whatever means we may seek to attain it.

COMMUNITIVE AND DISUNITIVE ACTS

A good or virtuous act is "communitive." By affirming the essential identity of the actor with those affected by the act, it establishes communion with essential being, which transcends the particularity and thus the isolation we experience from one another. An evil or sinful act by contrast is "disunitive." By invoking otherness, it repudiates and distances us from our essential nature. Selfless acts are communitive. Self-serving acts are disunitive.

If doing good brings us into communion and doing evil into disunion with essential being, then it is for us as moral creatures to establish criteria by which we gauge and guide our actions. We routinely judge real-world conduct all along the spectrum against the principles at the poles held to be universal. Anything of which we would predicate good or evil is never in fact purely so, but at best an admixture or tainted semblance of such principles, which transcend the particulars of experience and cannot pertain to them unconditionally. Furthermore, this polarity notwithstanding, good and evil in their purest form are not strictly speaking opposites if evil is nothing more than a denigrator of worldly good and does not itself mirror any aspect of essential nature. This softer polarity explains how we can legitimately exclude evil from God's all-encompassing purview. (In many faithlores, God does indeed assume destructive and patently evil forms.) For evil is not a true contrary on the same plane as good or God, or something unto itself rooted in a higher power of being, but rather a mere deficiency or contaminant of good as it manifests in the world.

The challenge of using such a measuring stick is compounded considerably as we factor in the myriad, often unanticipated, outcomes unleashed by our actions. You give a homeless woman a dollar for breakfast this morning (good), which she squanders on a bottle of Thunderbird (evil) that sends her staggering into traffic. The extent to which our efforts to promote the good reflecting essential intimacy succeed in thwarting (and thereby delivering us from) evil defy any clear and conclusive accounting. Nor can the transcendent core of communitive conduct be reduced to any temporal context of righteous behavior, even when the act is informed by it. As much as we weigh its ramifications — and for any consequential act we would be remiss not to do so — the actual effects of any act taken are, despite their existential significance, superfluous essentially. On that level the act ramifies presently and inconsequentially; any redemptive power it possesses lies only in the act itself. Some take exception with the notion of a single act at life's end, for example, with the power to eradicate prior sins, no matter how numerous and egregious. But primaversally no act is irrevocable or actualizes historically. A choice made at any given moment may be of precious little consequence historically, but none other save for the one at present resonates eternally. Every day is Judgment Day.

Far from lifting the burden on us to act mindfully and responsibly, this underscores the importance of evaluating every choice we make authentically and on its own merits. Only in the moment — so fleeting and elusive — do we partake of eternity.

WHY DOES GOD LET BAD THINGS HAPPEN?

It's an age-old theological poser and the atheist's ammunition of choice. It may also be the reason cited most by erstwhile believers for turning away from God. If God is good, then why does He allow bad things to happen? Why is there evil in the world? Certainly, if the world were as good and perfect as God, then it would be equal to God and not a lesser and contingent creation. But is that sufficient to explain the pain, suffering, and destruction that afflict us?

God admits and expresses all possible outcomes. He does not and need not decide among outcomes or choose which emerge. His omnipotence is His "omnipotential," His power to express and not to limit or exclude possible outcomes. When particular things happen, alternative (and some may judge preferable) outcomes emerge multiversally. The determinacy and distinct identity of any given universe and timeline are purely existential phenomena that define and delimit our experience. To imagine a God that fashions, presides over, distinguishes, and governs the sundry affairs of multiple universes (or even just one) is to view His essential and eternal being through an existential prism. That everything happens — and everything does happen — because of God does not mean that He acts or intervenes temporally. Intervention is a form of interaction, the modus operandi of beings within an actuality in which particular causes bring about particular effects. Lest we infer that by not so intervening God must be regarded as negligent, it may be said that through present causality He rather "subvenes" all-pervasively, but below the fray, if you will. As per the ontological argument, however, were he merged with or mired in nature, He could be neither source nor sovereign of it.

In addition, existentia, or obvents, are complex entities resulting from conceivably countless constituent outcomes. Consequences benign and tragic may befall them via the intricate web of interdeterminism woven by our choices and actions and the myriad interactions beyond our influence in the actualized environment. God enables but is not like us and everything else in the world complicit in this process. The bad things that He "allows" to happen emerge exclusively and irrevocably (and therefore to us regrettably) by means of the abridgment through which the prevailing actuality filters out alternative outcomes. But for God their being so never precludes their being otherwise. The patient that expires from the design flaw in the artificial heart valve enjoys a happier fate when the designer does not make the error or corrects it earlier, or the patient adopts a healthier lifestyle sooner and avoids surgery until the flaw is corrected. While such events are directed and restricted to singular outcomes within the prevailing actuality by antecedent causality, none is ever excluded essentially by any that has transpired emergently. What in particular we experience and how it shapes our existence to the exclusion of other possibilities does not in this view reflect premeditated divine intent or the totality of God's will.

Finally, the "goodness" or "badness" of the things we experience, like the acts we perform, is an empirical judgment made from an inevitably limited perspective. Is anything that happens unequivocally good or bad? Our hapless patient's demise is all but untimely for the next person, mercifully spared the device whose flaw has been exposed. No good-or-bad determination can ever be absolute or account for all the myriad effects and consequences on all affected parties. To consider whether ours is "the best of all possible worlds," as Leibniz believed, is to accept that such a determination is even possible or has any real meaning.

In summary, God wills and expresses everything that happens but does not orchestrate the particular things — whether we judge them good or bad — that happen to us within our existential context. The absolute extent of His will and determinism can be appreciated only in the multiversal context in which all possible outcomes are expressed. Thus when we assert that what happens is God's will, we are mistaken to exclude outcomes and eventualities that we do not ourselves experience. With regard to a particular universe like ours, His determinism does not entail restricting possible outcomes or conducting the business of antecedent causality. Cast in a more clinical light, the tranject does not "decide" unilaterally which reduction to express in a given environment until interfacing with or receiving input from that environment. One might therefore say that universally God's determinism is legislative rather than executive.

And that is precisely what allows us free will.

FREE WILL AND DETERMINISM

The constraints on us as existential beings are considerable. We are swept along from a past we cannot change to a future we cannot discern. We can act only in the moment, and no action taken can be taken back or rendered inconsequential. Nonetheless we are empowered to exercise our free will and thereby participate in the creation of our world and ourselves. This is a reflection — though a vastly impoverished one — of God's own expressiveness, and more than any other the way in which we are cast in His likeness.

God commands unlimited creative powers because primaversally all possible outcomes are eternally so. None excludes any other, and none is irrevocable. So it may have been for us in Eden. But, alas, our eviction from paradise meant giving up the amenities along with the accommodations. Our creative powers are drastically diminished because with determinacy comes determinism. As particular obvents actualize to the exclusion of others, the cascade of causality is set in motion. Our existential identity and environment are vulnerable to myriad consequences, mostly beyond our control, that effect and restrict outcomes and limit our freedom accordingly.

But not entirely. To exercise our free will is to resist the restrictions imposed by antecedent causality by directing our intentions and actions to promote particular outcomes and inhibit others. We leverage self-determination against determinism, present against antecedent causality, potentiality against actuality. By seizing the moment and embracing its eternal possibility, we seek to influence the prevailing actuality and loosen the shackles of existential being.

This struggle for self-determination, however, cannot be viewed as a renunciation of God's will. On the contrary, our efforts to shape the prevailing actuality, and with it our own destiny, are an invocation of essential being and an appeal to present causality. With every act of self-determination we enjoin and affirm God's will. Every such act is in this regard an act of faith. Faith holds us fast to the underlying absolute and immutable ground of being, where every possibility is imperishable, even as the relentless tide of becoming would uproot us. Whether we dub this faith religious or metaphysical or something else is immaterial. It rises anew in the form of hope from the ashes of disappointment and regret. It beckons us to seize the moment and participate in our own creation.

Some have taken the position that a multiverse precludes free will because your choice of mint-chocolate-chip ice cream is rendered meaningless by your choice of pistachio in a second universe and vanilla in a third. That is not so. Your willful actions define you only within your own universal context. Any multiversal expression of alternate choices also expresses alternate versions of you that differ and diverge from you in existential identity and have no bearing and no effect whatsoever on your existence. Only you live with and continue to be shaped by the consequences of the particular actions freely and willfully taken by you.

DESTINY AND RESPONSIBILITY

We cannot hold our Creator accountable for our fate or the fate of the world if His creativity does not involve micromanaging worldly affairs. We maintain that He need not and does not choose which particular outcomes emerge and thus which particular destiny befalls us. Such reasoning would seem to contradict the idea of preordination, which holds that — free will notwithstanding — we are guided by divine providence to follow one path and realize one destiny to the exclusion of any other, and that God knows it before we do.

How does this notion fare in this new metaphysics of ours? Certainly God expresses and thus has "knowledge" of every point on the path taken by us. But does that knowledge come "before" that point is reached; is it *fore*knowledge?

Recall our second globe analogy of the primaverse in which every point and path on the surface is eternally "active." Each possible outcome and thus sum of outcomes, or destiny, is timelessly viable and does not actualize, except universally, to the exclusion of any other. There is no "before" at which time there may be knowledge of something yet to come, nor "after" at which time some path may have been followed or point arrived at theretofore. There is only an eternal now encompassing all outcomes. Primaversally they express neither exclusively nor successively, as they do for us. Strictly speaking, the notion of *fore*knowledge or *pre*ordination of particular outcomes does not pertain because God in His omnipotence and omniscience conceives and perceives all outcomes in a single, timeless, all-encompassing act of creation.

It may be said that God knows everything that for us has happened and has yet to happen. Whereas we can acquire knowledge only of a particular outcome once it has emerged, i.e., after we have experienced it, God's knowledge is not limited to what has actualized for us or to when it has actualized. The idea that our lot in life is preordained (not to mention our "ultimate" spiritual fate predestined) captures some of this truth, but distorts it as well. God knows and wills our destiny in its entirety along with countless alternatives, but once the particular outcomes we experience have emerged, we are unable to experience any other.

Perhaps the biggest problem with the view that God has mapped out a particular destiny for each of us — and for all of us — is that it can be used, or misused, to let us off the hook in terms of our own accountability for what happens in the world. If preordained by God, then surely it is out of our hands and pointless to fret about the damage we may be doing through any actions of our own.

But what we do matters. Our actions have creative — and/or destructive — power by virtue of their consequences on the prevailing actuality. They culminate in particular and existentially irrevocable outcomes. We cannot foresee or control all of their ramifications. Nor can we bring infallible judgment to bear on the choices that guide them. In the absence of such a calculus, which would be tantamount to omniscience, we must assume responsibility for our actions commensurate with their potential impact on others and on the world.

With the gift of free will comes the burden of responsibility.

PRAYER AND MEDITATION AS COMMUNION

As emergent beings we are distanced from and yearn for reconciliation with our essential being. This alienation is reflected in our feeling of isolation from one and another, and from God. It may be mitigated by exercising our free will communitively, as well as through prayer or meditation, by which we seek guidance, atonement, enlightenment, or spiritual fulfillment.

Prayer often seeks not deliverance from but rather comfort or relief within the confines of our existential condition. Thus we may give thanks for outcomes experienced, ask forgiveness for actions taken and guidance for those yet to be taken, or even supplicate — like the football team that prays for victory — for desired eventualities. All of these instances are acknowledgment of our limited powers over the complex goings-on of the universe.

When prayer takes the form of a plea for divine intervention on behalf of the supplicant, it embraces the notion contested here of a God that intervenes in or willfully micromanages our temporal affairs. But this should no more than worship of a household deity or saint diminish or delegitimize the communitive intent or effect on the supplicant of such prayer. The invocation itself may be seen as having communitive value, regardless of the face given to transcendent being or the specific content if any of the prayer.

Meditation or meditative prayer rejects supplication or related content that anchors us in existential experience. The practitioner endeavors to free oneself from those moorings and seek interaction on a transcendent level as essential being. There is no attempt to dress God in our nature, but rather to surrender to His, which is ultimately ours as well. That this type of communitive exercise is more ambitious and elusive may explain why it is less commonly undertaken.

It should be noted that in both prayer and meditation the mind is directed (outwardly and inwardly, respectively) at God as an object even if our intention is to establish a relation whose aim is to dissolve and transcend that very relation in communion. Indeed it would be challenging if not impossible to conduct such an exercise or ritual without first establishing an objective and positing an object, though God is not one. It should be clear that God-as-object is thus a "placeholder" established for the purpose of any devotional undertaking, but *merely* a placeholder.

In any case the contrast between prayer and meditation can be extended to more general dispositions by which we may seek authenticity and communion in conducting our daily affairs.

We may lay claim to our creative power and harness our free will toward effecting better eventualities. Here we embrace and channel our own potential impact — often in resistance to that of countervailing influences — in shaping the world. We take exception with aspects of the prevailing actuality, even our own existential identity. We aim to effect change by asserting present over antecedent causality, and thereby invoke essential being. We are thus engaging in a kind of *communion by deliberate action.*

Or we may reject the significance or primacy of the outcomes we experience and gain a sense of detachment from them. Here we acknowledge that our underlying being and essential identity remain unchanged by and impervious to such outcomes. We more easily accept and even resign ourselves with relative indifference to the prevailing actuality. We celebrate the dominion of essential over emergent being. We are thus engaging in a kind of *communion by disengagement* from worldly affairs and even our own existential identity.

In these contrasting dispositions we may recognize the activist and the ascetic, the mover and the mystic. So too may we find ourselves gravitating to one or the other under different circumstances or at different times in our lives.

Communion is not the exclusive province of religious devotees or those who proclaim themselves spiritually inclined. The introspection, reflection, and "soul searching" we all engage in, the mental and physical as well as spiritual pursuits through which we strive for fulfillment and authenticity, and the actions willfully taken or declined every day of our lives may all have communitive effect by bringing us closer to one another, to ourselves, and thereby to our essential being.

THE SOUL AS ENCAPSULATED ESSENCE

Even as we emerge and abide as existential beings, the essential being from which we actualize is embodied, or "encapsulated," within us. An imprint or vestige of absolute, immutable, and indivisible essential being, this encapsulated essence is nothing other than the soul.

By this definition all things emergent have "souls." But perhaps in no other instance than ourselves do they have awareness of their plight as existential beings. Perhaps in no other instance has that awareness produced communitive principles like truth, fairness, justice, and the concept of an almighty God by which we may direct our will and to which we may devote our efforts. The embodied essence of a tree or a tapeworm is likewise distanced from God. But absent our highly evolved self-consciousness neither is likely to be consumed with or motivated by the feeling of alienation and yearning for redemption so salient and defining to our human being. This motivation and its potential for realization earn human being in Eastern faiths the highest rung on the ladder of possible incarnations — higher even than those divinities that inhabit the cosmos.

As vestigial or latent essence encapsulated in existence, the soul undergoes degradation from pure essential being. Within the existential confines of its host, individual and differentiated, it too becomes remote from and surrenders the desegregated unity of its original undifferentiated form and source. Despite such attenuation, the soul nevertheless maintains its identity with essential being and profoundly binds emergent being to it. Thus it inspires and enables communion, whose principal challenge is to overcome the isolation and differentiation we endure as existential beings, and recover the absolute intimacy of essential being.

This speaks to the apparent discrepancy cited in Hinduism between the Self intrinsic to every self — to which we may attain as a way of transcending our material existence — and that very Self as synonymous with God. Since there are billions of the former but one, and only one, of the latter, how can they be regarded as the same? If differentiation of the Self is a mere artifact of existence, however, then primordial Oneness is not fundamentally contradicted by a multiplicity of Selves.

Another idea common to Eastern religions sometimes considered problematic is reincarnation, in which the soul "returns" in another subsequent manifestation. If we think of an "incarnation" as an expression of essential being, then all existentia may be regarded as incarnations, each with its encapsulated essence as postulated here. We would not argue, however, that the same differentiation of essence is maintained or repeated from expression to expression in time, but rather that "re"-incarnations are the countless and multiversal expressions that issue timelessly from essential being.

WHENCE MORALITY

The impulse innate to the soul for communion with essential being gives rise to morality in an existentially and socially circumscribed context. That impulse is relentlessly opposed by the condition of individuation and otherness that defines our existence, and finds satisfaction only insofar as it succeeds in mitigating and transcending it. Communion in this context requires that we repudiate otherness even as we recognize it, and the impulse for communion finds expression in compassion, whereby we feel for and identify with others. Our sense of morality — of fairness, equality, tolerance, justice — emerges in the social reciprocity of compassion that keeps otherness at bay and prompts altruistic or communitive behavior, as summed up by the comprehensive moral directive **Do unto others as you would have others do unto you.**

While moral principles like justice and equality are general and absolute in that they transcend particular instances and qualifications, they are not strictly speaking essential because they pertain only in the existential context of reciprocity and relativity in which they have meaning and purpose. They are universal (and multiversal) but not primaversal. As directed away from otherness and thus toward essential — by way of social — communion, they may be regarded as "adessential" precepts. All moral principles aspire to essential purity under existential restrictions and are thereby adessential.

Rights may be framed to uphold these principles, as well as laws to proscribe their violation. Such laws reduce and concretize general principles to specific prohibitions of particular antithetical acts (***thou shalt not kill***), for which punitive measures deemed appropriate and commensurate (***an eye for an eye***) may be exacted. Social institutions are set up to protect principled conduct and to deter and punish unprincipled behavior. Thus the moral imperative of society is to defend principles held inviolable and the practical business of morality the legislation and enforcement of rules and regulations established to that end.

Society, like the individual, is morally deficient or corrupt when it fails to honor the impulse for communion and the principles derived from it. Society, after all, is no less than the individual an expression of essential being, if not a more fully realized one to the extent that it mirrors essential integration by desegregating its constituents, and provides the context as well as the mechanism for altruistic and communitive conduct.

Are the principles of morality and the commandments that direct us to heed them social constructs or divine ordinances? To be sure, they are conceived in a social context and have the effect of maintaining social values and social order. Insofar as they are mandated by the soul's impulse for communion, however, the purpose ultimately served transcends any social context, and they are essentially motivated if not divinely ordained.

GOD'S GRACE: BESTOWED OR ATTAINED?

The subject of God's grace has been among the most divisive and misunderstood in Christian theology, with no consensus reached after centuries of consideration as to whether or not we can cooperate through good works toward our own deliverance. If God's grace is unilaterally conferred and can only be received and accepted or rejected by us, does it then follow that we cannot merit His favor through our own willful deeds and devotion?

Many Protestants hold per Martin Luther that faith is the acceptance of justification, a complete and binding act of forgiveness imparted by God's grace for all acts committed and yet to be committed by us. Thus while neither faith nor justification can be revoked, any effort to contribute to our own salvation is in vain because our existential separation from God makes us sinners in spite of them. In the Roman Catholic view our virtuous works may build upon a "prevenient" grace and accrue toward justification by God's decisive grace, with or without our avowal of faith. Sins are discrete acts, which may be pardoned, and faith an intellectual decision, which may be reversed, as may justification in the case of mortal sins.

Grace may be understood in the context of this metaphysics as the effulgence of God's eternal expression, including his will and love. It is unambiguously receptive because its direction is and must be ever outward from God. We cannot reciprocally act on or affect God, who is not an object and whose infinitude timelessly encompasses our every possibility. While communion with God loosens the oppressive grip of existence on our essential being, we cannot conclusively overcome our separation from Him to the extent that we remain confined to and identified with our minds and bodies in time and space. (Bodhisattvas and yogis purportedly elude such confinements though they tarry in this world by attaining spiritual liberation on the plane of divine consciousness.) At the same time righteous intentions and actions, contemplation and atonement arrived at of our own free will are inspired by nothing less than God's effusive grace. Thus to act communitively is to accept God's grace; to act disunitively is to reject it. In the latter sinful behaviors we are complicit in abetting our sinful state of separation from Him. Grace cannot be — nor ever need be — reversed or revoked, since God admits contradiction, so primaversally exculpation and condemnation (were God to entertain something akin to our projection of these) are not mutually exclusive as one or the other may preside presently according to our earthly conduct. As eternal and sweeping as His expression, God's grace does indeed apply to all actions taken and yet to be taken by us and is not contingent on any particular action in time. In Jesus it shines with undiminished splendor — received directly, embraced unambiguously, and realized utterly through his every deed and ultimate sacrifice such that the Christ and the sacraments invoking Him become the vehicle by which we may in turn receive it, and through it salvation from ignoble finitude. Thus He is not only the messenger but also the message, whose new being shepherds and transforms our own.

The confusion over this issue is understandable given a faithlore based on notions of time and space and relationality from which we can produce an edifying allegory, but by which the ineffable mystery of transcendence cannot be circumscribed. It portrays in the past a lost paradise in which newly created man enjoys a being untainted by the desolation and despair of becoming. It portrays in the present a state of exile that is our punishment for transgressions committed by our forbears and perpetuated by our own sinfulness. It portrays in the future everlasting salvation or perdition as deemed appropriate by our Lord and Judge. It portrays in all three a god above and apart yet acting in time, as we do, and with whom we stand in a conventional if atypical relation of subject to object.

In truth separation from and salvation by God are equally timeless cohorts of His primaversal expression. God's grace and our faith are the push and pull of essential being toward communion. The characterization of grace as definitively and unilaterally bestowed seems incurably at odds with the idea of spiritual fulfillment as an objective freely and willfully chosen by the aspirant, and attained (and *ret*ained) by means of virtuous industry. But there is no conflict between the granting of grace by God and its self-selecting and self-directed acceptance or rejection. Grace is bestowed essentially, ever-presently, and without prejudice, yet the privilege is enjoyed only by those heeding its call for authenticity and rectitude. It is not an exclusive membership, but an eternally open invitation. It bars no soul, no matter how wretched, at any time in any universe from the righteous pursuit of redemption.

CREATION NOW

When we introduced the ontological argument from contingency for a first cause of existence, we accepted as axiomatic its necessity, but only by wresting such fundamental being itself *from* existence, and thus contingency. Indeed, this notion of non-existential being had already been established with the designation of essential being at the outset of this investigation, which we then further identified with God the Creator, whose expression of emergent being may be understood *as* creation.

Such creation must be distinguished from the *inception* of our universe that set time and space and the galaxies in motion, and launched the chronology and actuality that defines our existence. It is not *initial* but rather *present creation* (from which present causality is extrapolated vis-à-vis particular existentia), an eternal act in which primaversally all of time is now and essential being in its unbridled expression beholden to no chronology or actuality but only timeless possibility. Nor is this idea alien to theologians and philosophers, a number of whom held analogous views before, during, and after biblical times (not to be dissuaded by a literal reading of Genesis or other creation myths).

Present creation in no way excludes but subsumes and subordinates creation in time from the tick before the tock of the existential clock. (You will recall that essentially no event including the first is indelible, or closed off to alternative and infinite expression.) It clearly precludes, however, the notion of a creator so acting in time and completing the work of creation as an artist completes a painting. That creator could have abandoned us, as some have argued He has. But the God of present creation is no more remote today than when the stars twinkled anew or man first gazed upon them because creation is now and His act of creation eternal.

Rest assured that God did not set the universe in motion so He could give it His blessing and tend to other matters. While the universe is indeed imparted with a kind of self-perpetuating momentum through antecedent causality, or the cascade of cause and effect, no single outcome can emerge except through present causality as a direct expression of essential being. That is the mechanism of timeless creation from an absolute prior ground, without which we would be cut loose from our essential being and swept away by the tide of existence — with no presence, no self-determination, no soul.

CREATION EX NIHILO

It is not easy to put a familiar face, or any at all, on a creator who labors beyond time and space and existence. While no doubt an extreme makeover for the iconic Deity of poesy and popular imagination, this view of creation may come into clearer focus through a comparison with Christian orthodox doctrine, which embraces the notion of "creation ex nihilo."

According to creation ex nihilo, God deliberately and willfully fashions the universe and everything in it from nothing. In common with our view, God is ontologically prior to the universe and assumes the role of a first cause necessary for and essential to its existence. Yet in contrast with our view, God is distinguished from the stuff of creation insofar as the world is fashioned *from* nothing *by* God, who is therefore implicitly *other than* nothing. It is important to point out that "nothing" must be understood here as not only the *absence of* existence but also the *potential for* existence, which is precisely what it becomes in God's hands and by God's will. Such a "nothing" has conceptual without existential content. (Consider by analogy that zero has no numerical value yet anchors and imparts value to all positive and negative numbers, and is itself equal to the sum total of their values.) So we can safely say that prior to existence God *is* and nothing *is* but that God *is not* nothing, and moreover stands in a subject-object-like relation to it.

Our view, on the other hand, rejects this distinction and relation. It requires that as the absolute ground of existence, the Creator be wholly identified with the primordial and ultimately irreducible *stuff of creation*. The world is not fashioned by God from something else, but emerges immediately and directly from God. To complete the identity, as the source of existence and not Himself existent, God is not *some thing* but that very *no thing* from which creation arises. Thus we have not ultimately departed from (and if anything more fully embraced) creation ex nihilo. The related notion of "emanation ex Deo" proposed by Plotinus firmly establishes this identity in the form of the transcendent and abysmal One from which existence issues and which is therefore beyond and not itself existence.

This remains entirely consistent with the dichotomy initially drawn between existence and essence. Existentia acquire their objective character, or "somethingness," with the spacetime determinacy assumed in the existential-empirical context. As the pre-actualized potentialities that express them, essentia may themselves be characterized by their "no-thingness." The expression of existential by essential being is thus precisely creation from nothing. This brings us full circle to the amended interpretation arrived at earlier of the ontological argument for a first cause: Absent intrinsic necessity, existence must arise from that which is not itself existent and thus contingent.

We end the chain of contingency, in other words, only with a first cause that is not *some thing*, defined by its relation to something else and thus not itself absolute, but rather *no thing*, of unconditional presence and unqualified possibility. Such a creator, and none other, possesses intrinsic necessity and so does not emerge from some prior ground because it does not emerge at all and requires nothing other than or prior to itself in order to be.

III.

"The greatest enemy of any one of our truths
may be the rest of our truths."

— William James

TRUTH

Sagacites

You seem lost in thought this fair morning, young Aptaeon.

Aptaeon

Forgive me, revered Teacher. Despite your cogent arguments, I struggle to grasp how objectivity belies rather than divulges ultimate Truth.

Sagacites

The mind is inured to convention. Tell me what troubles you.

Aptaeon

The natural sciences take pains to devise experiments that yield precise objective measurements. Do they not?

Sagacites

They do.

Aptaeon

In this way they seek to light the way to ultimate Truth. Do they not?

Sagacites

They do.

Aptaeon

And the observations so made are held to be far more reliable by virtue of their sensitive instruments and controlled conditions than any you or I might make.

Sagacites

Agreed, young Aptaeon. A worthy and scrupulous discipline is this science.

Aptaeon

Does it not follow that the truths revealed by means of this exacting method are the most infallible and unimpeachable, and thus the highest to which we may attain?

Sagacites

You would put us philosophers out of business, young Aptaeon! Consider the empirical method you champion. Does it not share as its basis the very same relation of subject to object as our everyday experience?

Aptaeon

It does.

Sagacites

And yet is not its aim to gain knowledge of the object as it is in itself, uncolored by experience and thus uncompromised by that very relation?

Aptaeon

Hence the pains taken to overcome the limitations of the casual observer and obtain findings more accurate and truer than ordinary experience yields.

Sagacites

Can any pains taken overcome the limitations of observation itself if the empirical relation and thus all empirical findings are confined by their relative context to contingent and qualified truths?

Aptaeon

Again my head spins with confusion!

Sagacites

Not long ago we arrived at the realization that the absolute eludes determinacy in space and time, which characterizes only to the relative. Do you recall?

Aptaeon

I shall not forget it.

Sagacites

Was this realization not arrived at by purely subjective means, with no reference to any object to which you the subject stood in relation?

Aptaeon

It was.

Sagacites

Yet you would now insist that absolute Truth be divulged objectively and beholden to determinacy?

Aptaeon

It cannot be. I am clearly mistaken.

Sagacites

Is science as an empirical undertaking then not confined to relative truths objectively gleaned and determinately gauged?

Aptaeon

It would seem incontestable.

Sagacites

And does not scientific objectivity carry the same taint of relativity as our own meager and fallible experience?

Aptaeon

No matter how precise its measurements, it is indeed so tainted. Yet what are we to make of recent experiments designed to circumvent the observer?

Sagacites

A commendable yet ironic attempt to "de-objectify" the empirical object, as it were. What sort of insights have they produced?

Aptaeon

Those so peculiar and vexing as to confound painstaking observation and ordinary experience alike.

Sagacites

Does this not support our original contention that the empirical relation veils and denies access to absolute Truth, unbounded as it is by the contingency and relativity that circumscribe our own limited experience and existence?

Aptaeon

No other conclusion seems warranted, revered Teacher. My head spins no longer. I am greatly relieved!

Sagacites

Then let our shingle hang a while longer, young Aptaeon. We philosophers may yet be of service.

THE PROBLEMATIC LEGACY
OF THE PRIMACY OF EXISTENCE

T HIS INVESTIGATION HAS MADE EXPLICIT the contingent and consequently subordinate nature of existential being. Beginning with the disclosure of indeterminacy underlying being as experienced, we have considered and embraced a notion of fundamental being that cannot be accurately characterized or confined by existential qualifications, and therefore transcends not just experience but existence itself. Even our metaphysical orientation as self-determining beings is to invoke transcendence in order to mitigate existence and its constraints on us.

This line of reasoning is at odds with a longstanding (though not always explicit) ontological tenet that existence is metaphysical ground zero, so to speak. You may recall the premise of Anselm's ontological argument (with which we took exception) that that which exists is "greater" than that which does not. Ibn Sina, who put forth the argument in its original form, likewise clung to the primacy of existence by maintaining that God's essence is nothing other than existence, though not bestowed or imparted but intrinsic, and so qualitatively different from that of contingent being. Despite the strain it may exert on logic, as both of these formulations attest, the assumption of existential supremacy is not easily abandoned.

This assumption confuses more than the issue of God's, or essential, being, as discussed earlier. It also legitimizes a propensity in our intellectual tradition to equate and thus conflate the qualified "truth" of empirical fact, or what happens to be (in existence), with absolute truth, or what is necessarily and eternally so (in essence), and by extension to ascribe to fact the significance and sanctity of truth.

But empirical truth is not and cannot be absolute. Fact changes with perspective in place and time. It's a fact that the sun revolves around the earth until a preponderance of evidence demonstrates otherwise. It's a fact that the ivory-billed woodpecker is extinct until multiple sightings are captured on film in the deep woods of Arkansas. It's a fact that a man on death row is a murderer until a DNA test overturns his conviction. It's a fact that alcohol increases the risk of breast cancer until a study shows that red wine actually reduces it. Facts historical and scientific can only aspire to absolute and unequivocal certainty. They are subject to the inevitable relativities and limitations of contingent existence, and so must be continually refined and revised, and ultimately replaced, as clearer and wider and sharper perspectives emerge. Existence, while determinate, is nonetheless qualified and possesses no intrinsic necessity, and fact may therefore only approach truth. Facts held to be "true" are approximately or arbitrarily rather than unconditionally so, and such "truth" (much as the "good" discussed earlier) is an imperfect semblance of truth.

This is not to diminish the power of fact, which points

to and draws us ever closer to truth. The problem arises because the assumption of existential primacy promotes twin misconceptions (or, really, two sides of the same misconception) — first, that empirical truth is fundamental and thus tantamount to essential truth; and second, that essential truth is existentially accessible and can be validated empirically.

As we shall see, these misconceptions confuse how we think about and even conduct science and religion, and have fostered an ill-founded antagonism between them. But first we shall examine the tension between essence and existence, truth and fact, rooted in our own religious tradition.

THE CHRIST PARADOX

Christian faithlore comes directly and powerfully to grips with the dichotomy and underlying unity between existence and transcendence. In Jesus, God manifests in time and flesh as emergent being, and as such assumes all the contingencies and vagaries of existence. Kierkegaard spoke to the impenetrability of religious and essential truths — and this one in particular — which the intellect may perceive as paradoxical, offending our understanding and challenging us to overcome our repulsion of the incomprehensible by way of faith.

The story of Jesus is so compelling precisely because Jesus' destiny, like ours, is a function of his own willful actions and creative participation in the context of the actions of others and consequent outcomes beyond his control. In existential form he relinquishes divine omniscience and omnipotence and acquires mortal vulnerabilities. His humanity and his struggle to shape himself and the world in the face of adversity are what make his choices and deeds exemplary and his suffering pathetic and redemptive. Like Jesus, all of the characters in the story are accountable for their actions and participation in steering the events that unfold. Were Jesus or God the Father pulling every string and directing the players and events, the story would lose its power and pathos.

Rare if not unique among faithlores, the Gospels give us multiple accounts of the story, providing a distinctly historical-factual flavor — its events related and recorded as witnessed by contemporaries. This is entirely consistent with the theme of God as personified in the historical figure of Jesus. An historical Jesus not wholly identified (like Buddha or Zoroaster) with an absolute creator may have religious value on par with other faith-defining figures, but nothing short of God coming into actual existence so fully captures the principal themes of communion, salvation, and redemption on which this particular faith is based.

Because overtly mythic faithlores — while they depict a particular setting and revolve around particular characters — do not ask to be read as history, they can be simply embraced and "believed" for their thematic and metaphorical value, which is understood to transcend the particulars of the story. In Christian faithlore, by contrast, the central theme and metaphor of transcendence in existence, God in man, as expressed by the historical-factual narrative device of the Gospels, compels the reader to embrace as fact and history the particulars of the story. That is why the literal as opposed to the allegorical embodiment of God in Jesus is widely regarded as the non-negotiable, acid-test belief among the Christian faithful.

Accepting this shift from the metaphorical to the historical has radical implications. Primarily, as historical-factual accounts, the Gospels could not be tantamount to absolute and necessary truth since the story they tell resides squarely in the realm of existence. Empirical fact, unlike truth, cannot be free of contingency or the relativities of experience. What actually and precisely happened in this or any instance never can be ascertained with unequivocal certainty. Yet believers and dogma are likely to defend every detail of the Jesus narrative as necessary, absolute, and inviolable truth by virtue of the essential nature of divinity, even to the extent of arbitrating any differences or discrepancies we may find in the accounts. Does this not directly contradict the historical and existential premise of the story as underscored by the absence of a single definitive account?

Moreover, once God enters existence and history in the form of Jesus, in this view, every eventuality is subject to antecedent causality. Anything can be otherwise and nothing is necessarily so. Going still further, alternative admissible outcomes may emerge multiversally, meaning the life of Jesus may unfold otherwise in parallel scenarios, in which Judas, for example, does not betray him, or Pilate arrest him and dispatch him to Calvary that fateful Friday. (We must, however, acknowledge the "bookend" events of Jesus' life, his conception and resurrection, whose supernatural portrayal would demand in contrast with the intervening events — or for that matter events as we understand them in general — direct and extraordinary intervention from God the Father, exempting them from existential contingency.)

We may consider that Jesus, his essence encapsulated and differentiated by dint of existence — but in no way impure or adulterated like ours — acts under every conceivable circumstance with absolute compassion and justice and virtue, but those circumstances nevertheless remain as variable as the actions and reactions of others. Accepting Jesus as an existential being in history and in fact, and the Gospels as historically accurate accounts, means accepting the events related as contingent (i.e., they could have transpired otherwise) and rules out elevating to the level of necessity the particulars of the story.

Alternatively, we may understand that in its unique employment of *fact as metaphor* (perhaps overlaying some historical reality), the narrative remains nonetheless ultimately allegorical or analogical. We may then view its particulars in terms of their transcendent metaphorical or symbolic value rather than their historical accuracy, so that the integrity of the narrative is not contingent upon its being taken literally. That this latter interpretation may be seen as diminishing rather than preserving the truth of the narrative is symptomatic of the tendency discussed earlier to assign supremacy to existence rather than essence. Indeed, it may be a very consequence of this faithlore to promote that tendency.

Unfortunately, the misconception snowballs. First, it prompts us to dismiss as having lesser value than facts truths related through symbolism or metaphor, as in other faithlores that do not insist on factuality. Second, it compels us by extension to seek and claim factuality in overtly allegorical texts, including arguably the Old Testament, again in the belief that fact is paramount and tantamount to truth, and that empirical validation reigns supreme. Notice that with the advent of the gospels and a "New Testament," the earlier bible inherits the retronym "Old Testament," extrapolating and imposing a factual, testimonial, and evidentiary significance where little or none may be appropriate or have applied previously.

This tension between the metaphorical and the factual is

part and parcel of the pervasive and problematic concern of Christianity to reconcile the transcendent with the existential. Nowhere is this more apparent than in the sacrament of the Eucharist, in which the consecration of bread and wine as expressed and effected through the metaphor *This is the body and this the blood of Christ* does not merely symbolize but invokes the Real Presence of Christ *as* corporeal being, which in turn (per the foregoing discussion) invokes the presence of God *in* corporeal being. In both cases the essential truth and power of the metaphor transcends and trumps the factual truth of the empirical object, be it the bread and wine, or the historical person of Jesus.

Kierkegaard shared the keen insight that a subject considering an object cannot acquire complete or accurate knowledge of its being because both are in a state of becoming, or if you will, their being is not fully expressed. When God is objectified in Christ, His being is revealed in becoming, but only in a very conditional sense. God is *not* an object and His being cannot be circumscribed or contained existentially by becoming — hence the paradox, which must direct us beyond the objectification and its particulars, where we cannot go via ordinary experience, toward the transcendent truth.

The great truth of Christian faithlore lies in the redemptive power of communitive action as exemplified by Jesus, and the ultimate primacy of eternal over temporal being. The great power of Christian faithlore lies in a story told as an historical account that gives such resonance, palpability, and accessibility to this truth. But in some sense, ironically, its message may be undermined and even have disunitive consequences when taken purely literally ("as gospel"). The zealous defense of factuality — that these events really happened in just this way — as having primary significance is overplayed to the detriment of the narrative's value. Problems ensue when the particular facts exclusive to this narrative are regarded as fundamental rather than the eternal and immutable truths they are meant to reveal.

MORE ON FACT AND TRUTH
IN SCIENCE AND RELIGION

Christian theology has a rich heritage of rationalism that cross-pollinated with and fueled the burgeoning empirical and natural sciences. Copernicus and Mendel, among others, were monks who examined the heavens and earth in an effort to uncover and understand the miracles of creation. For centuries the greatest minds straddled religion and science with equal devotion and passion. But the conflating of essential truth and existential fact has produced deadly clashes at times and an uneasy truce at best between religion and science. In one episode of milder friction, scholastic theologians were ridiculed for their alleged efforts to determine how many angels can dance on the head of a pin. This criticism, apocryphal or not, points to the misappropriation of an empirical mode of investigation for inquiry of a decidedly non-scientific nature.

Both science and religion are dogmatic to the extent that they adhere to principles and assertions embraced and defended by their respective establishments. Challengers invariably encounter resistance. But because science is a progressive enterprise, it contains a mechanism for, tolerates, and ultimately demands paradigm change. Driving this mechanism is the recognition that scientific fact is not absolute and immutable but aspires to, approximates, and approaches the underlying truth with ever greater accuracy through ever more precise empirical observation and measurement. It's an iterative process. That our solar system has nine planets is a fact recently revised as new data have prompted a reassessment of the status of Pluto. Religious dogma, on the other hand, does not tolerate or accommodate challenge or change because its principles and assertions are held to be incontrovertible as they express (to the extent possible by the language of contingent existence) transcendent truths. That the Father, the Son, and the Holy Spirit are One (though not the same!) is true by definition and cannot be challenged empirically because no amount of evidence can be brought to bear on proving or disproving it.

Assertions factual and spiritual alike may be viewed as "beliefs" when embraced with conviction by those who make or ascribe to them. But the only legitimate criterion for factual beliefs, which pertain to the world of experience, is empirical evidence, or rational judgment based on it. And the only legitimate criterion for spiritual beliefs, which pertain to transcendental matters outside the realm of experience, is faith, or rational judgment based on it. Conflict arises when the proper distinction between statements of contingent fact and transcendent truth is disregarded.

Earlier we deemed the assertion "God exists" inadmissible because although articulated as a factual statement it does not qualify as such since it eludes empirical determination. Equally problematic are legitimate factual statements propounded as necessary truths. These include assertions like "The world was created 6,000 years ago." Factual assertions attain the status of fact only by virtue of empirical evidence. The preceding statement no longer meets the criterion of fact and is at the same time inadmissible as a statement of transcendent and necessary truth.

These matters, however, are not always so cut and dried. Factual assertions are commonly made "on faith" in the absence (or denial) of credible or sufficient empirical evidence. It is an inescapable limitation of contingent existence that empirical fact is not and cannot be absolute and thus absolutely unequivocal. There will always be those who cling with fervent belief to discredited factual assertions in the face of overwhelming, unambiguous, and (to the extent possible) incontrovertible evidence to the contrary. The blur in the boundary may stem in part from the common pedigree of theology and science in classical rationalism, which defended physical and theological contentions alike solely by means of argument. This no longer meets the burden of proof for science, whose truths have gained the "hardness" of fact with empirical validation. But it has not changed for religious ideology, which must rely on rational argument to delineate, interpret, and formalize doctrine. Moreover any assertion that reveals essential nature also belies it, as no proposition can adequately capture the transcendent truth to which it speaks. It does not necessarily follow that it therefore has no value or yields no meaningful insight into reality.

That fact is not the province of faith should not, however, lead us to conclude that faith must be absent from science. (Don't forget Copernicus and Mendel, or Einstein's admonition that "Science without religion is lame; religion without science is blind.") The same faith we discussed earlier in the underlying truth that anchors our being — and to which we appeal unceasingly in our struggle to define ourselves

— applies no less to science. There have been more than a few skeptics who believe that the scientific (as well as metaphysical) pursuit is a waste of time because the truth will remain forever beyond our grasp. But the eternal presence of truth is precisely what motivates and inspires science, however fully we are ultimately able to grasp it. If there is a trap here, it could only be baited by the misconception that truth, which is transcendent, can be wholly and finally explained and contained by scientific fact. Fortunately, that mystery creates precious little deterrence and all the more allure for the curious and quixotic practitioners of science. As a result we gain ever greater, if never absolute, illumination of the wonders of our world.

Not only is science a faith-based enterprise, but receptivity and revelation are crucial to its success. The miracles of creation disclose themselves to us through a dialectic of doubt in which currently held beliefs are questioned and new possibilities entertained. Here it is the challengers of dogma, oftentimes those with the greatest irreverence, who achieve the greatest triumphs.

Throughout history science and religion have been strange bedfellows and strained adversaries. Under pressure from ecclesiastical authorities, Galileo recanted his ardent refutation of a geocentric universe. In deference to the religious establishment, Darwin delayed for many years the publication of *On the Origin of Species*. To this day religion and science continue to clash on important issues. Could the tension between them be mitigated through keener discernment in distinguishing matters of contingent fact from transcendent truth?

As of late a subject of controversy has been the belief that "Life begins at the moment of conception." This is a case in point because within the scientific community the validity of this assertion remains very much open to question. Should not all of us — religious leaders in particular — welcome elucidation on this matter of fact as a way toward greater ethical clarity in areas as heatedly polarized as abortion and embryonic stem cell research? Will this assertion a century from now prove as quaint and misguided as "The sun circles round the earth"?

Only time will tell.

ASSERTIONS OF PRESENCE

Let us return briefly to the argument made earlier that facts can be true only in a qualified sense. This may have given you pause if it occurred to you at that very moment that the fact that "I am reading this book" is not qualified in the same way or to the same degree as those statements given as examples of empirical fact. You have greater confidence in its veracity because you are living it right here, right now.

Descartes similarly stood his ground in his *Meditations* when he imagined the possibility that an evil genius had conjured up everything he perceived, prompting him to doubt its reality and strip it all away until the only thing of which he claimed absolute unshakeable certainty remained: *I think, I am, I exist* (the so-called "cogito").

In the view of this metaphysics an "assertion of presence" must be designated an exceptional type of statement of fact as it refers to and is rooted in the creative moment of the obvent in emergence. While, unlike the denuded Cartesian cogito, your assertion that "I am reading this book" is cloaked in sensory perception — of the words on this page, your easy chair, the dog at your feet — it nevertheless arises from a more fundamental and pre-sensory "awareness of presence," of being in this moment reading this book, which in turn stems from your emergence in that capacity directly and unmediated from essential being. This is the window on eternal possibility in which you harness your intention and action toward self-determination. That this window is open when we make assertions of presence distinguishes them from empirical statements based solely on perception, observation, measurement, or even personal memory.

We depart in this understanding from Descartes, who sought to establish in his thought experiment God's existence by way of his own, or more accurately we depart from Descartes' own appraisal of the exercise. For he was encountering, as in a true meditation, not existence, from which the exercise seeks disengagement, but transcendent presence underlying and independent of existence.

Even though it may be regarded and interpreted and validated as a statement of empirical fact and likewise has no intrinsic necessity, an assertion of presence possesses by contrast a transcendental component because regardless of its cognitive content the fact reflected in your statement is anchored by your presence in essential being. It is "truer," so to speak, or closer to essential truth than other statements of fact, not because you experience it for yourself (seeing is believing), but because your presence in the here and now (*being is believing*) tethers it to primaversal expression.

THE TRUTH, THE WHOLE TRUTH, AND NOTHING BUT THE TRUTH

We may now delve deeper into the distinct nature of truths underlying not only scientific and religious propositions but all assertions and concepts. We shall specify three orders of truth that invite closer examination: the first corresponding to our temporal existence and experience of it, the second to our timeless presence rooted in essential being, and the third to essential being itself in its transcendent and absolute necessity.

First is the empirical "truth" (and antithetical falsity) of contingent fact that pervades our ordinary experience and shapes our understanding of the world. Because it is acquired by means of a relation or mediation between subject and object, our conception is a representation derived but removed from the being of the object itself. Moreover, as touched upon earlier, since the interaction between subject and object occurs at a given point in time in a ceaseless state of becoming, such conception has the further deficiency that it cannot capture the being of the object in its entirety as fully expressed, or, for that matter, independently of the fluctuating relativities of emergent being in an actualized environment.

All of this suggests that the notion of an unambiguous "objective" truth to which empirical fact aspires is unattainable if not altogether illusory. But it would be more accurate to characterize empirical truth as precisely objective and recognize that we regularly attain objective truth — yet are mistaken to identify its objectivity with the unequivocal or

absolute. An objective truth outside the flux and fray of temporality and relativity, and exempt from the qualifications
imposed by them, overreaches itself. Objectivity is a feature
of existence and a mechanism of experience that cannot be
extricated from the subject-object relation or the broader
existential-empirical context.

Let us take a closer look at how empirical truth is ap-
propriated, as illustrated in Graphic A, below. We acquire
our conception of a thing along a "vector of experience" by
means of a dynamic *to*, which is its objectification, and *fro*,
which is its apprehension. The conception thereby acquired
is clear and distinct and comprehensible, but for the rea-
sons stated above ultimately "unfaithful" to the being of the
object. Even so, its acquisition effects the becoming of the
subject and evolves its constitution, and is therefore subjec-
tively and existentially formative.

The second order of truth coincides with our timeless
presence, which tethers and draws us to our essential being
even as it eludes our existence. Thus we may refer to it as
adessential truth. Here the object of experience is absent
from the relation, which is directed at the transcendent, or
God. The conception discloses along a "vector of engagement" by means of a dynamic **inward and toward** that is
an enstatic relinquishment of existential self, as the relation
or mediation dissolves itself in identification and communion. While unintelligible or non-rational, the conception
disclosed is nonetheless "faithful" to the essential being
from which both subject and object of the prior relation (and
everything else) emerge. This insight, or **intimation**, is sub-

jectively but not essentially transformative or existentially deterministic.

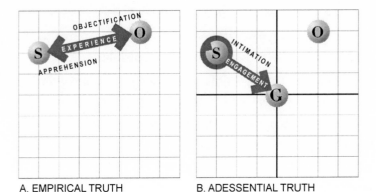

A. EMPIRICAL TRUTH   B. ADESSENTIAL TRUTH

Graphic B shows the relation and dynamic between the subject and God, whose presence is indicated at the intersection of x and y axes at coordinates 0,0. While those coordinates themselves have no value, they impart absolute value to anything in the overall field (not to be construed as spatial). In contrast, the subject and object in Graphic A have presence solely in terms of their relation to one another; they are adrift in relativity. This is intended to illustrate that while God Himself possesses no objective or existential content, He anchors existence and its relativities in the absolute.

The third and ultimate order of truth is essential truth. Here the only relation is Self-relation, or pure subjectivity. The dynamic is expression, and the conception is neither acquired nor revealed but rather timelessly generated along infinite "vectors of emanation." In this case the conception is not merely tantamount but ontologically **equivalent to** the unabridged being itself as fully and manifoldly expressed. And thus knowledge — which is primaversally Self-knowledge — of the truth is nothing other than the Truth. This Self-relation is neither formative nor transformative of the Subject, as either would contradict its absolutivity.

Empirical truth governs our existence but lacks the absolute if ineffable sovereignty of essential truth. Between the two lies the gateway order of adessential truth that grants mysterious passage to redemption and reconciliation. To assert the legitimacy of one order of truth to the exclusion of another, or arbitrarily enforce its rules where they have no jurisdiction, does nothing to advance the quest either for intellectual or spiritual fulfillment.

PONDERING ESSENTIAL TRUTH

What manner of truth could represent fundamental constituents of being that we have portrayed as intimate despite
their autonomy and absolute despite their indeterminacy?
Such curious and profoundly counterintuitive compatibili-
ties are not likely to cooperate with any existential syntax.
What's more, if determinacy is the gauge of empirical truth
alone, and the only gauge of it, how can we take it away and
be left with anything like truth, much less absolute truth?

Let's not forget that we examined at the outset certain
statements that transcend the contingency and particularity
of empirical truth. Analytical statements true by definition
like "a triangle is three-sided" and "man is a sentient being" hold true in all possible worlds, whether or not any
triangular things or humans happen to exist in them. We
have also looked at analytical statements with no possible
worldly reference like "God is good" which must therefore
be regarded as metaphorical or analogical.

Are we not within our rights to call these familiar and
straightforward propositions essential truths? They meet the
burden of necessity, and inasmuch as they make no specific empirical reference, they even sidestep determinacy.
As pure concepts and defining principles, they call to mind
Plato's Forms, his take on essentia, of which the particular
objects of experience are but a meager semblance.

On the other hand one might gripe that they are mere
tautologies. They hardly capture, moreover, the complex,
indeterminate, and unintelligible character ascribed here to

essential being. But then how can a proposition really do that?

Putting analytical statements aside, we equate what is true with what *is*. With two modalities of being to contend with, however, we must acknowledge Bill Clinton's notorious insight (quite legitimate here) that precisely what that means depends on your definition of "is." In the realm of contingent existence "is" means *that which happens to be*, which we evaluate in contradistinction with *that which happens not to be*. Such contradistinction does not apply essentially, where "is" encompasses all that is admissible and possible, or *that which can be* (existentially).

Following this line of reasoning, propositions like "the traffic light is red yellow green" may warrant our consideration. The statement makes no sense empirically, which indeed it should not, and is consistent with our understanding of essential being. The subject is actualized being but the predicate is *essentially* true of it in a way that an empirically appropriate predicate in the statement "the traffic light is red" cannot be.

Predicating anything other than metaphorically *of* essential being is quite another story. As suspected the propositional syntax breaks down altogether when we venture into the primaverse due to the absence of an individuated subject of which anything might be predicated. Because the tranject is not a sensible object of experience, it cannot fulfill the role of a propositional subject. Indeed what is true essentially is not true *of* something as it is empirically. When the obvent emerges and assumes determinacy, truth "adheres" if you will to the *this* or *that* which actualizes. Essentially, however, truth is not adherent but inherent; it does not *re*present one finite aspect of reality or another to one observer or another at one time and place or another, but presents it wholly, unconditionally, and absolutely.

Such truth eludes the grasp of reason and solicits the embrace of faith.

*"A little philosophy inclineth man's mind to atheism;
but depth in philosophy brings about man's mind to religion."*

— SIR FRANCIS BACON

ESSENCE

versus

EXISTENCE

REDUX

T HIS METAPHYSICS BEGAN with the classical dichotomy between being as experienced and being as it is in itself, and then took an iconoclastic turn by limiting the notion of existence exclusively to the former. This interpretation of reality is likely to raise eyebrows, not least of all when applied to God. As pointed out earlier, "existence" is traditionally understood both conversationally and ontologically to have the same meaning and breadth of meaning as "being." If something *is*, then it *exists*. Some may take the position that this synonymy is inviolable and that so radical a departure as the one taken here is unwarranted and indefensible, or even a deliberate attempt to stir up controversy.

No such attempt has been made. The understanding expressed and the categories established developed logically and organically from this investigation. The truth and value of this exploration (if it is deemed to have any) emanate largely though not exclusively from the idea that existence is solely a contingent and qualified modality of being that neither contains nor pertains to transcendental being.

The claim that God, and essential being, is necessary but cannot be said to exist is no glib and hollow assertion. Because our understanding of existence is inseparable from our experience and context and contingency as beings in space and time, to extend the notion and purview of existence beyond them must therefore ultimately be recognized as what is truly unwarranted and indefensible, despite any potentially unsettling or counterintuitive implications. It is a classic case of the wrong categories forcing the wrong conclusions. To have sidestepped or soft-peddled this insight by drawing the dichotomy of being between "emergent" (rather than "existential") and essential *existence* (rather than "being"), for example, would have been to shield from the probing light of our investigation something directly and undeniably in its path in order to let a longstanding misconception live another day.

Instead we exposed an eminently questionable (and in this view misguided) propensity to "existentialize" transcendental being that pervades centuries of metaphysical and theological inquiry and informs in no small way our prevailing worldview. This insight challenges us to let go of assumptions so deeply held that they are scarcely questioned, much less disputed. But these assumptions are part of our ideological inheritance and accepting them as given is not sufficient justification for holding them sacred. We think how we think because we stand within an ideological tradition — and standing *within* it naturally limits our perspective. It pays to bear in mind that our tradition of "realism" supplanted another tradition of realism, that we now call idealism. In that tradition, with its Platonist heritage, reality is understood in terms of universals or essences whose being imbues and subordinates particular things. Late medieval thinkers led by Ockham reacted against this orthodoxy and lobbied for a more Aristotelian view that acknowledges only the reality of individual things and regards essences as conceptual but in no way substantial.

The triumph of this latter outlook colors in no small way our view of the world, and of God, to this day. Thus our "realism" is more precisely *nominalism,* in which reality is solely the province of particular things and certitude comes only from our experience of such things. God Himself takes on the objective character of an individual entity and that becomes the nature of the relation in which He stands to us. This undercuts religious positivism gained through a non-sensory, non-objective participation in divine Being, and leads directly to empirical positivism, and, from there, to scientism. That this bias emerges out of the philosophical and theological rationalism that also spawned science explains why the debate between atheists and believers has taken place in that oddly overlapping space, and why opposing sides have consented more often than not to terms that call for something akin to empirical validation of God.

The foregoing investigation prompts us to ask whether such nominalistic positivism has become too extreme, too radical, and as a consequence too restrictive. Our all-existence-no-essence ideology has increasingly marginalized (if not malnourished) any underlying spiritual or essential component of our being, or declined to recognize it in the first place. Demystification is de rigueur. Yet, as we have seen, science itself has secrets to tell about what arguably lies beyond its pale that call into question its own final authority. Could deeper insight into the being that lurks under the cover of our existence impart new meaning and relevance, transform our understanding, inspire communion, or awaken devotion? Could we renew our acquaintance with God in such a way that neither casts Him in our likeness nor casts Him out altogether? Could the conventional wisdom and prevailing pieties yield to a swing of the ideological pendulum away from the dispassionate empirical positivism we so fervently embrace? Throughout our history that pendulum has never stopped swinging, after all. It is not likely to do so now.

Finally, this disquisition should be read as an entreaty not to surrender our values, or give up our beliefs, or compromise our principles, but rather to recalibrate our thinking, vested though we are in it, and guided as we must be by that highest of all principles: Truth. For surely it shines even now on this ever so remote, ever so improbable, ever so narrow sliver of the multiverse we call our own.

GLOSSARY OF TERMS

Absolutivity The independent character of tranjects, or essentia, as defined intrinsically rather than by their relation to other tranjects.

Actualization The emergence of being with spacetime determinacy in a spacetime environment.

Adessential The nature of a principle or precept that is not itself purely essential but aspires to and enables movement toward essential being.

Antecedent Causality That which effects the consequent outcomes or eventualities that forge the existential identity of the obvent.

Assertion of Presence A statement of fact distinguished by a transcendental component whereby it is anchored in the here and now.

Christ Paradox The conflict between the historical-factual device central to the Christian narrative and divine necessity.

Cognitive-Sensory Apparatus The prism of sensible intuition and cognition through which we perceive and process reality.

Communitive The character of a selfless intention or action and its consequences that brings us closer to one another and our essential being.

Contingency The dependence on a prior cause in order to be as something is and in order to be at all.

Decoherence The apparent collapse or reduction of the complex indeterminate state exhibited by the quantum wavefunction into the simple determinate state observed and experienced by us.

Determinacy The nature of existential being to possess a particular state with discrete properties and definitive values.

Determinism Generally, the effect and power of external causes to direct outcomes. Also, the doctrine that events and human actions are so directed.

Disunitive The character of a self-serving intention or action and its consequences that distances us from one another and our essential being.

Emergence The emanation of actualized being as an expression and manifestation of essential being.

Emergent Being Existential being from the standpoint of its emanation from the more fundamental modality of essential being.

Empirical Fact The qualified and contingent truth of existence arrived at through and validated by experience.

Empirical Object The object of experience and observation as accessible to us in existential form.

Encapsulated Essence The trace of essential being, or soul, that lingers in us as an impure semblance bound to and drawn to its original source.

Ensistence, or Inherence The state of essential, or non-existential, being.

Essential Being, or Essence The fundamental modality of being that transcends being as experienced and from which it emanates.

Existential Being, or Existence The emergent and contingent modality of being that constitutes our existence and experience.

Existential-Empirical Context The interdependent domain of existence and experience within which our own being is delineated and operates.

Expression The creative behavior and activity by which essential being generates and manifests as existential being.

Faithlore The principal narrative and set of beliefs proprietary to an established religion.

Immediate Outcome An existential outcome as it emerges directly and without intermediate contingency from essential being.

Indeterminacy The fundamental nature of essential being to retain a complex state that cannot be characterized by discrete properties and definitive values.

Individuation The segregated character of obvents whereby their identities are discrete and differentiated.

Interdeterminism The comprehensive codependence of existentia as agents and products of the chain of cause and effect.

Intimacy The desegregated character of tranjects whereby their identities are undifferentiated and evince unity in multiplicity.

Intimation The immediate, non-relational, participatory intuition of essential or divine being that cannot be acquired as knowledge or through ordinary experience.

Mediate Outcome, or Consequence An existential outcome as effected by antecedent causes and interactions in the prevailing environment.

Multiverse The sum of self-contained, actualized spacetime environments and histories that constitute the complete expression of essential being.

Necessity The characterization of that which must be rather than may be, and must be as it is rather than otherwise.

Obvent, or Existentium The actualized entity of existence and experience characterized by its spacetime extension and determinacy.

Present Causality That which effects the immediate outcomes that establish the emergence and presence of the obvent.

Primaverse The pre-emergent, spacetime-transcendent realm of essential being.

Reduction The transition from a complex original state to a simpler derivative state, or the result of such a transition.

Relativity The character of obvents as existentially defined by their relation to other obvents and the actualized environment.

Superposition The complex nature of pre-emergent being whereby it at once possesses multiple states and properties.

Threshold of Emergence The boundary postulated for illustrative purposes at which existential being actualizes as an expression of essential being.

Tranject, or Essentium The pre-emergent constituent of essential being characterized by its spacetime transcendence and indeterminacy.

Transcendental Being Essential being from the standpoint of its transcendence of spacetime and the existential-empirical context.

Transcendental Object The thing-in-itself as opposed to being as experienced, or the empirical object.

Universe A single, self-contained, actualized spacetime environment characterized by its unique chronology and history of outcomes.

ACKNOWLEDGMENTS

No less challenging than getting these words on the page has been getting these pages in front of readers. You are turning them now only because of people who cared enough to support this project and its author.

An early draft would still be gathering dust on the shelf had Michael Posner not championed this work. He prevailed upon colleagues to peruse it, vet it, even pass it along to editors. Whenever agents and publishers overlooked it, Mike prompted me to persevere. His belief in it sustained my own.

Others near and dear earn mention here for never questioning (though surely doubting!) my sanity, or objecting to the time, energy, and resources devoted to such an improbable undertaking. These indulgent relations include my wife Carla Posner, my associate PJ Posner, and my parents Gerta & Jerome Posner, to whom I dedicate this little book.

This has not been exclusively a family affair. I am indebted to Michael diCanio for help with design and marketing, among other things, and to Alan Klein and Alexander Neubauer for their sage counsel. I hope that L. Aryeh Kosman, my philosophy advisor way back when, will accept my gratitude for time taken and feedback given.

Many whose names do not appear on this short list also deserve thanks for their encouragement and efforts on my behalf. They have them.

CPSIA information can be obtained at www.ICGtesting.com
Printed in the USA
BVOW060151250612

293449BV00001B/2/P

9 781936 940240